"When trying to find texts to compare Kgositsile with one thinks of Pablo Neruda of Chile, García Lorca of Spain, Agostinho Neto of Angola, Okot p'Bitek of Uganda, and Thomas McGrath of the United States. . . . There is something magical in the way the personae of these poems seemingly start in one direction, reverse, or deviate to side paths, and then deftly start in an entirely different one to begin anew on another plane of reality. This is the work of a poet hearing his own muse and inventing an original expression as medium for the oracle."
—Sterling Plumpp, foreword to *If I Could Sing*

"[Kgositsile's] poems transcend the superficial definitions which some might attempt to make on the basis of quick-draw ideologies, tactics and postures from yesterday's conferences, and keep their fingers on the pulsations of the Black soul history. That emotional history, with its consequent cry for steadiness and action, for undeviating clear-sightedness, for rejection of death, in its range of reference and feeling, jumps forth in these pages as truly deep Pan-Africanism—the truly joining thing."
—George Kent, introduction to *The Present Is a Dangerous Place to Live*

"What Kgositsile has to say is too urgent for the conceit and fanciful ambiguity of literary artifice."
—Chinua Achebe

"I would say that [Kgositsile] is a 'master,' if it were not for my belief that no one 'masters' *any*thing, that each finds or makes his candle, then tries to see by the guttering light. Willie has made a good candle. And Willie has good eyes."
—Gwendolyn Brooks, introduction to *My Name Is Afrika*

For Willie Keorapetse Kgositsile

BY KOFI ANYIDOHO

Somehow   You Survived.
You Survived Your Exile Years

Went Back Home to Old Comrades
You Thought You'd Never See Again.

Went Back Home to Lay Your Exile Tears
to Rest Among the Graves of Old Warriors

Share Your Dreams of LiberationTime
with a Generation Too Young to Know
the Taste of Blood from Bitter Battle Days

Bitter Bleeding Battles Fought So Long
Over a Nation Torn   Apart   Between
HerSelf   and   The Colours of Her Skin.

KEORAPETSE KGOSITSILE

KEORAPETSE KGOSITSILE

Collected Poems, 1969–2018

Keorapetse Kgositsile

Edited and with an introduction
by Phillippa Yaa de Villiers and
Uhuru Portia Phalafala

University of Nebraska Press / Lincoln

The University of Nebraska Press is part of a land-grant institution with campuses and programs on the past, present, and future homelands of the Pawnee, Ponca, Otoe-Missouria, Omaha, Dakota, Lakota, Kaw, Cheyenne, and Arapaho Peoples, as well as those of the relocated Ho-Chunk, Sac and Fox, and Iowa Peoples.

The African Poetry Book Series is operated by the African Poetry Book Fund. The APBF was established in 2012 with initial support from philanthropists Laura and Robert F. X. Sillerman. The founding director of the African Poetry Book Fund is Kwame Dawes, Holmes University Professor and Glenna Luschei Editor of *Prairie Schooner*.

Library of Congress Cataloging-in-Publication Data
Names: Kgositsile, Keorapetse, author. | De Villiers,
Phillippa Yaa, editor. | Phalafala, Uhuru Portia, editor.
Title: Keorapetse Kgositsile : collected poems, 1969–2018 /
Keorapetse Kgositsile ; edited and with an introduction by
Phillippa Yaa de Villiers and Uhuru Portia Phalafala.
Other titles: African poetry book series.
Description: Lincoln : University of Nebraska Press,
2023. | Series: African poetry book series
Identifiers: LCCN 2022017512
ISBN 9781496221155 (paperback)
ISBN 9781496222091 (epub)
ISBN 9781496222114 (pdf)
Subjects: BISAC: POETRY / African | LCGFT: Poetry.
Classification: LCC PR9369.3.K4 K46 2023 |
DDC 821.914—dc23/eng/20220412
LC record available at https://lccn.loc.gov/2022017512

Set in Adobe Garamond by N. Putens.

CONTENTS

EDITORS' NOTE

IN THE ORIGINAL . . .

Immersing ourselves in Kgositsile's oeuvre, we note the repetition of lines, phrases, and concepts as the poet proceeds through successive publications, which Phillippa Yaa de Villiers describes as a palimpsest. Although these repetitions remain consistent, there are certain poems that Kgositsile seems to have reconfigured into different clusters or suites of poems, possibly reframing his poetics to meet a different historical moment and a new readership.

Notable examples of these include the grouping of poems in *The Present Is a Dangerous Place to Live*. In its original publication in 1974, in the suite "There Are No Sanctuaries except in Purposeful Action," the first part of the poem is untitled, but by the time it is republished in *If I Could Sing* (2002), it has the title "Wounded Word, Insane Song," which is reproduced in *Homesoil in My Blood* in 2018. The poem "Notes from No Sanctuary," which was originally published in *My Name Is Afrika* in 1971, appears in *The Present Is a Dangerous Place to Live* as part of the "There Are No Sanctuaries except in Purposeful Action" section, after the five-poem suite.

It is exactly reproduced in *If I Could Sing*, where Kgositsile is possibly creating a different effect, one that is more in keeping with the historical moment and a different audience: this was the third publication on South African soil after decades of exile during which South Africans had been largely unable to obtain his work. As historian and biographer, a poet's words immortalize the subjects of his attention, in this case the activists Kate Molale and Duma Nokwe. Two separate poems, entitled "Kate" and "My Sister," lamenting the death and celebrating the life of his comrade Kate Molale, appear in *Somehow*

We Survive (1982) and recur as one poem called "Kate" in *This Way I Salute You* (2004). In its first publication in *Somehow We Survive*, "A Luta Continua" begins with a tender address to its subject Duma Nokwe, "Duma, child of my mother" whereas in subsequent publications, notably in *If I Could Sing* (2002), it begins with a lament and a call to action.

The title poem of *Spirits Unchained* appears as one of the four-part suite "Point of Departure: Fire Dance Fire Song" in *My Name Is Afrika*.

On her field research in the States, Uhuru Phalafala discovered Kgositsile's MFA creative component submitted to Colombia University in 1970, in the form of the manuscript "My Name Is Afrika." The unpublished manuscript as dissertation is originally dedicated to Malcolm X and Frantz Fanon. Poems that did not make it into the final published collection are included in the "Uncollected" section at the end of this volume.

INTRODUCTION IN TWO MOVEMENTS

1. Today We Move: Departures into Creativity

PHILLIPPA YAA DE VILLIERS

Keorapetse William Kgositsile was, outside of his homeland, South Africa's most celebrated poet. Described in O. R. Dathorne's *African Literature in the Twentieth Century*, "Kgositsile is not merely an Afro-American poet or an African poet. He fuses the two roles into one, and the two experiences are one. His work shows that he is never at loggerheads with the Black society he describes. His is the truly universal Black voice."[1]

Literary scholar Uhuru Phalafala and I started working on locating the texts, most of which were published in the United States, in 2017, with his full knowledge and blessing. On January 3, 2018, he died, before seeing the final manuscript.

I first encountered Kgositsile through his poem "Red Song" during the hopeful 1990s, when apartheid was being dismantled (and being replaced with the neoliberal economic policy—but that's another story). Keorapetse Kgositsile came back to South Africa in the early nineties, and his collections *When the Clouds Clear* (1990) and *To the Bitter End* (1995) became immediately available. True to his artist personality, he began collaborating, and the eminent vocalist and composer Vusi Mahlasela set "Red Song" to music. The opening lines are sung in the mournful, radiant voice of the griot:

> Need I remind
> > Anyone again that
> Armed struggle
> > Is an act of love

It was a call to action that traversed decades of struggle. This "act of love," expressed so simply, asks its readers to embrace the contradiction of the returning soldier with compassion and gratitude for the work done to liberate the country. The poem exemplifies Kgositsile's undisputed ability to honor the truth in all its complexity, with a musicality that draws on the repository of memory and history, rebuilt through the rhythms and cadences of jazz.

Born on the outskirts of Mafikeng and raised in Sophiatown, Johannesburg, Kgositsile grew up freely interacting with Black intellectuals and journalists, jazz musicians and artists of the vibrant cultural nucleus. He joined the African National Congress (ANC) as the apartheid government was brutally enacting its policies—the Sharpeville massacre (March 21, 1960) was the cue for the ANC to embark on armed struggle, and he was instructed to leave the country. He lived in various newly liberated countries in Africa, eventually arriving in the United States. During this time he began writing and reciting poetry, and contributed to journals such as *Negro Digest*, the *Liberator*, *Freedomways*, and other Black journals that were pushing the boundary between scholarship and creativity. He taught at various colleges in the States, including Queens College, Bennett College, State University of New York at Stony Brook, University of Denver, Wayne State University, New School for Social Research, University of California at Los Angeles, and after 1975 at the Universities of Dar es Salaam, Nairobi, Botswana, Zimbabwe, Zambia, and Fort Hare. Many South African writers and poets—such as Lewis Nkosi, Lefifi Tladi, Peter Abrahams, and Es'kia Mphahlele—became ambassadors for the armed struggle, building relationships with communities of resistance overseas, but Kgositsile's influence exceeded the literary field to contribute to culture more broadly, especially education and, of course, politics.

In *Grounds of Engagement: Apartheid-Era African American and South African Writing*, Stéphane Robolin centers Kgositsile in what he calls "Black transnationalism"—those engagements, circulations, migrations, and practices that "imagine arrangements of space and place that articulate modes of belonging not siphoned through the rubric of the nation-state."[2]

In Kgositsile's magisterial poem "No Serenity Here," composed in 2008 in response to South African people's xenophobic attacks on African nationals, he writes, "In my language there is no word for *citizen*.... That word came to us as part of the package that contained the bible and the rifle."

Robolin's contribution to the scholarship is a detailed examination of epistolary relationships developed over the twentieth century, notably between Langston Hughes and Richard Rive. Kgositsile's poetics expand the boundaries of language, place, and tribe, digging deeper to the lode of culture, which, in the socialist tradition, is a site of resistance and expression, and a vibrant repository of knowledge and debate not to be separated from historical material conditions.

Exile was already a part of ordinary life for Black South Africans, a continuation of the colonial invasion that dispossessed them of the land, relegated Indigenous languages and cultures to curiosities, and enslaved all able-bodied people, decades before the apartheid policies came into effect. Sol Plaatje recorded in *Native Life in South Africa*, "Awakening on Friday morning, June 20, 1913, the South African native found himself, not actually a slave but a pariah in the land of his birth."[3]

In his *Reflections on Exile*, Edward Said described exile as "an unhealable rift between the self and its true home."[4] A number of the poems in *My Name Is Afrika*, particularly the "Death Doses" suite, and the first section of *The Present Is a Dangerous Place to Live* speak to an exilic sense of hopelessness and alienation. But Kgositsile's writings and performances produced a community of ardent supporters and colleagues who found resonance in his riffs and expressions, and courage in his calls to action. His stature, particularly in terms of the diaspora, was a direct result of his belief in the principle of continuity between Africa and Black folks that lived everywhere on the planet. Tlhalo Raditlhalo notes in his chapter, "Writing and Exile," in *The Cambridge History of South African Literature*: "At Lincoln University in Pennsylvania he chose to immerse himself in this history of black America and in this way attained what he refers to as 'emotional placement' within literary production in the United States. As he explained in an interview[,] emotional placement for him was about 'one's orientation to sound and its effect and everything around them in an environment they are in.'"[5]

Besides the famous admiration for all things American that Africans had built up over the nineteenth and twentieth centuries through church, politics, culture, and fashion, the love story between the urbanizing African and the African American worldview found expression through culture, particularly jazz, a central theme in Kgositsile's oeuvre. Notable scholarship that explores Kgositsile's relationship to jazz include M. F. Titlestad's *Making the Changes: Jazz in South African Literature and Reportage* (2004). His love of jazz found its form in many tributes to the musicians who were interpreting their "here and now" with the resonances of Africa. His reading ear heard a "future remembered" in Nina Simone, whom he celebrated in his poem "Ivory Masks in Orbit":

ebony lady swims in this
cloud like the crocodile
in the limpopo midnight
hour even here speaking
of love armed with future
memory: desire become memory

Kgositsile's fascination with jazz informed not only the content of his poems but also his creative process. In an interview with K. Mensah Wali in *Sampsonia Way*, Kgositsile stated, "I approach my writing like that. I do my thinking away from writing, so when I sit down to write poetry, I take my solo. I literally approach it like a musician approaches his solo. I don't think, I write. Until it comes out, I don't know what's going to be there any more than the next person."[6]

This extraordinary vulnerability found its form in a creativity modulated by the values of his pan-African background, his political ideals, and his unapologetic subjectivity. These sentiments are eloquently articulated in his poem "There Are No Sanctuaries except in Purposeful Action . . . Two":

At the sound of the insane who think themselves sane
death's certain laughter eats away the vein of a whole
generation, leaving a legacy of spiritual and mental
bankruptcy, and decay, for the next. Violence, then,
documented past any argument by thousands of instant
deaths in terror-stricken township nights, is turned

inward. In piercing daylight too if you die you die.
We were so cool, we thought, shrouded in some shit
straight out of the pages of some american magazine

At times irreverent, Kgositsile was circumspect about identity politics when
it froze or demobilized minds bent on change. With work opportunities at
various universities, he was able to expand his contribution from writing and
performing to influencing pedagogy and supervising students. In this way, he
found himself at home.

He started producing poetry during the 1960s after arriving in United
States during a time of political volatility and Black solidarity, which found its
creative expression through the Black Arts Movement, where he played various
important roles, inspiring and critiquing activists with words of encouragement
or timely actions that supported them as they were responding to racism and
rebuilding community with Black arts at the center of the academic project.

Spirits Unchained appeared in 1969 and *For Melba* the following year;
both were met with enthusiastic acclaim. The former was published by the
then-fledging African American press out of Detroit, Broadside Press, edited
by the late legendary Black writer and editor Dudley Randall. The latter was
published by Third World Press out of Chicago, also a new independent press
for Black poets led by Black Arts Movement poet and activist Haki Madhubuti.
Both publications served to establish the authority of Black-owned, Black-run
cultural production houses.

Traces of the esteem Kgositsile garnered exist in paratexts, which are of
interest because they speak to the values that brought him closer to his col-
laborators and provide texture to notions of a culture of resistance. South
African poet, activist, and scholar Ari Sitas observes in the foreword of *When
the Clouds Clear*, the first Kgositsile collection to be published on South
African soil: "I think Kgositsile's poetry is . . . an emotional bond between the
urban rhythms of a dispossessed South Africa and the expressivity of a black
limitation of Chicago's ghettoes."[7] Kgositsile was barely thirty years old when
Gwendolyn Brooks wrote, "The young want to move and they want everything
else to move—including poetry. Willie Kgositsile's poetry lunges, strains its
muscles—and barks or howls or richly murmurs or screams."[8] Despite his

youthful success, his humility in the face of language was celebrated by noted poets, writers, and scholars of literature. George Kent introducing *The Present Is a Dangerous Place to Live* (1974) wrote, "Since Kgositsile remains humble in the presence of his people, he reflects a powerful fusion of the lover-warrior-revolutionist. His desire for a one-to-one communication with people is a part of his style and manner."[9]

Commenting on the intimacy of Kgositsile's political vision, Chinua Achebe observes in the foreword to *Places and Bloodstains* (1975), "What Kgositsile has to say is too urgent for the conceit and fanciful ambiguity of literary artifice."[10]

With his radical response to the African American struggle that resonated so much with his own struggle against apartheid, composing poems that spoke to the charged political situation—such as "When Brown Is Black," "Brother Malcolm's Echo," and many more—his voice was recognized and claimed by his adopted diasporic community.

Kgositsile's poems wove continuity between people and places, bonding and refiguring the struggles, claiming beauty as a human right, an aesthetic of radical love, and always celebrating connection: "Distances separate bodies not people" ("The Elegance of Memory").

Kgositsile's irritation with the Anglocentric thought of the white liberal literary mainstream is palpable in his foreword to the anthology *Somehow We Survive* (1982), edited by his close friend the great blues poet Sterling Plumpp: "South African literature, in many African languages with varying concerns of form and content, has a long rich tradition.... Despite the insistence of white liberal patrons who feel that if you are black and not writing in English, you're not writing at all, there are many more writers—poets, novelists, dramatists—in South Africa who write in their native languages than those who write in English."[11] Although he wrote in English, he was "taming English to speak Setswana," in a sense filtering the idiom of his mother tongue into the collective resource that is English, reclaiming language to assert himself as a political being in full possession of his intellectual, emotional, and spiritual faculties.

As a mentor he was unsurpassed, offering guidance, notes, gentle but pointed reprimands, and participating wholeheartedly when invited. For several years he served as a mentor at Khanya College, the oldest independent workers' college in South Africa. In 2009 he led a delegation of poets on a five-city tour of the

UK, publishing "No Serenity Here" for the first time in the tour's anthology *Beyond Words*, which is introduced by the legendary Black publisher Margaret Busby. His presence in the 2010 *No Serenity Here: An Anthology of African Poetry* translated into Mandarin, commissioned by the artist, industrialist, and philanthropist Xiancheng Hu, endorsed and supported the effort to offer African literature to a new audience.

It is with great pride and joy that we offer you this comprehensive collection of Kgositsile's poems. This volume contains, with very few exceptions and to the best of our research skills, all of his published work in the order of the collections that he produced over his fifty-year career. Like any jazz musician, Kgositsile had his own idiolect, licks and riffs, retaining lines, fragments of rhythms, and verses when building new poems, making of his own work a palimpsest. For example, the poem "Lumumba Section," which is a stand-alone poem in *Spirits Unchained* (1969), is one part of a three-part poem in *My Names Is Afrika* (1971). Also, four or five poems from a previous collection will appear in the next, so we trust that scholars of his work will forgive the fact that we have not preserved the integrity of the collections by repeating poems that appear in subsequent publications. Your reading will be different, hopefully equally valuable and pleasurable.

In a world where the diversity of human intellectual resources of language and culture are under threat from corporate Anglocentricism, Kgositsile's oeuvre is enduringly relevant, a bridge between the abject losses from colonialism and the resilience of people who resolutely remake the world in sound and action, endlessly regenerating the shades of an African linguistic tradition at the center of humanity. It is intended to inspire change: a poetry that continues to move, a movement that revives itself in poetry.

NOTES

1. O. R. Dathorne, *African Literature in the Twentieth Century* (London: Heinemann, 1980), 215.
2. Stéphane Pierre Raymond Robolin, *Grounds of Engagement: Apartheid-Era African American and South African Writing* (Urbana: University of Illinois Press, 2015), 6.
3. Sol T. Plaatje, *Native Life in South Africa* (Portland OR: Mint Editions, 2021), 186.

4. Edward W. Said, *Reflections on Exile* (Cambridge MA: Harvard University Press, 2000), 173.
5. Tlhalo Raditlhalo, "Writing and Exile," in *The Cambridge History of South African Literature*, ed. David Attwell and Derek Attridge (New York: Cambridge University Press, 2012), 420–21.
6. K. Mensah Wali, "'This Is Who I Am.' A Conversation with Poet Keorapetse Kgositsile," *Sampsonia Way*, June 25, 2012, https://www.sampsoniaway.org/literary-voices/2012/06/25/%e2%80%9cthis-is-who-i-am-%e2%80%9d-a-conversation-with-poet-keorapetse-kgositsile/.
7. Ari Sitas, foreword to *When the Clouds Clear*, by Keorapetse Kgositsile (Fordsburg, South Africa: Congress of South African Writers, 1990), 4.
8. Gwendolyn Brooks, introduction to *My Name Is Afrika*, by Keorapetse Kgositsile (Garden City NY: Doubleday, 1971), 1.
9. George Kent, introduction to *The Present Is a Dangerous Place to Live*, by Keorapetse Kgositsile (Chicago: Third World Press, 1974), i–ii.
10. Chinua Achebe, foreword to *Places and Bloodstains: Notes for Ipelang*, by Keorapetse Kgositsile (Oakland CA: Achebe Publications, 1975), 7.
11. Keorapetse Kgositsile, foreword to *Somehow We Survive: An Anthology of South African Writing*, ed. Sterling Plumpp (New York: Thunder's Mouth Press, 1982), xi.

2. The Light That Does Not Flicker

UHURU PORTIA PHALAFALA

Assembled here are the collected works of a cultural worker and statesman whose words are a clarion call to our deepest humanity and consciousness. They come to us in these dire times marked by crises of the human spirit, by gargantuan human greed bent on impaling our collective lives. They guide us toward ethics of care through radical empathy and revolutionary love that propel us to activate our innate instinct for human dignity and self-determination. The potential of his words to move us to purposeful action is dramatized by the ancient well from which they are drawn, enshrouded in prayer and ceremony whose fire illuminates our journey forward. We are called to move and be moved, to rise and meet ourselves, to dream as a collective, and to honor the memories of dream weavers in our desire for full humanity. This book is a tapestry woven by Keorapetse Kgositsile—dream keeper, ancestor, and guide.

Kgositsile published his first collection of poetry in the United States of America at the end of the turbulent and swinging sixties, a decade that, while positively disruptive in the larger Black world, was blanketed by totalitarianism in his native country of South Africa. Mapping his development to the grand and overdetermined regime of apartheid would be an injustice against this prolific writer who cut his teeth as a journalist in the urban upheavals of 1950s Johannesburg, characterized by the political and cultural vanguard of Black modernity. Importing a distinct sense of community, culture, and customs from rural Mafikeng, concretized in his domicile environment of Dithakong, where he was born in 1938, Kgositsile shuttled to Johannesburg in 1951 a knowledge of himself enriched by the invaluable teachings of his grandmother Madikeledi and his mother, Galekgobe. They asserted the primacy of Setswana language as a central component to his identity that must necessarily be utilized in countering the inherent erasure of British colonial education. These matriarchs insisted on the use of only Setswana at home, disassociating with the English language as one that arrived here on the ship. In a sense, the image of the ships instilled an ocean consciousness in Kgositsile from a young age, registering ships as ominous figures of violent acculturation. These womenfolk who raised Kgositsile in the absence of his father are central to his cultural and political consciousness for they modeled "homeplace as a site of resistance" (bell hooks). These formative years render veritable brushstrokes in the portrait of this writer as a young man, and his four-suite poem, "Point of Departure," published in *My Name Is Afrika* in 1971, bears witness to Madikeledi's wisdom, converging it seamlessly with that of key political figures in the Black world.

Kgositsile learned resistance from home and, while operating within circuits of nationalist and decolonial politics that were notoriously patriarchal and androcentric, was unapologetic in citing his grandmother and mother as sites of political education. In his interview with Charles Rowell of *Callaloo* in 1973, Rowell asks Kgositsile to talk about his early experiences, particularly those that had an impact on his writing. Kgositsile responds: "The earliest memories go back to two very strong women—my grandmother and my mother—in that order. Practically everything I write is tied up with some kind of wisdom I got from them in that hostile environment."[1] Proper credit has to be given to these women for his stature as a formidable cultural and political figure, academic, and statesman. Their knowledge system was deployed by Kgositsile in his formulation and enrichment of the Black radical imagination that spanned variegated geographical, conceptual, ideological, and pedagogical spheres. They instilled in him that a dream is not a dream if not a dream of the community. This education was instrumental in immersing him within the larger politics of the African National Congress in the 1950s as that liberation movement represented the dreams of the collective and the unified struggle to make those dreams a reality. His signal contribution to the ANC's revolutionary vision is his interweaving of culture and resistance, the pen and the AK47, inspired by Amílcar Cabral to assert the problem of liberation as the problem of culture. Kgositsile wrote, "In the beginning is culture, and in the end it's also culture."[2] His approach to decolonization was as much a cultural as it was an armed struggle, for he knew that any fashioning of a liberated future must necessarily deploy history as foundation lest the origins of our history be forever ascribed to the arrival of those ominous ships his grandmother warned him about.

In this sense we cannot offer a satisfactory reading of Kgositsile's work without factoring in this genealogy that converged his dreams of political freedom with the dreams of the communities he fostered on his exilic journeys, and the role of literature in articulating and enacting that convergence. By the time he was instructed by the senior leadership of the ANC to leave the country to avoid the mania of apartheid's dragnet post–Sharpeville massacre, Kgositsile was steeped in revolutionary fervor. His lacerating political analyses had been sharpened by training on the job as journalist at the leftist newspaper *New Age* (known as *Guardian* pre–Treason Trial), birthed out of the cauldron of ANC's 1952 Defiance Campaigns. There he had been mentored by Alex La Guma (who was stationed in the Cape Town office) and Ruth First, the editor of *New Age*. To contextualize *Guardian/New Age*, all its editors—Ruth First in Johannesburg, Brian Bunting in Cape Town, Govan Mbeki in the Eastern Cape, and M. P. Naicker in Durban—were defendants in the 1958–61 Treason Trial. Soon after Kgositsile left, Ruth First was the first detainee of the newly constituted Ninety Day Detention Act.[3] They were not just journalists but also political activists. This matrix of politics and culture is what distinguishes Kgositsile from his contemporaries who were (in)famously part of the *Drum* generation of writers, whose legacy is blemished by their contempt for active engagement with racial politics.[4] Their interstitial lives between domestic Black and white worlds, bohemian lifestyle, and the rejection of imposed insular homeland politics and its Indigenous languages as protest against apartheid's retribalizing project in their making of urban identities, all diverged from the political furor staged by the ANC, and by association, Kgositsile. While he also rejected the countryside and its tribalism, he committed himself to a unique project of finding continuity between the cultural imperative, his emerging urban identity, and later diasporic identity. This commitment is central to his appraisal by literary critics as a bridge between Black South Africa and Black America.

When Kgositsile arrived in the States in 1962, via Dar es Salaam, on a scholarship funded by the U.S. government to Lincoln University, he was extremely knowledgeable about politics of nonviolent resistance and the indefensible violence white supremacy responds with, as he had witnessed first-hand during the Sharpeville protests. He had been privy to the clandestine talks on adopting armed struggle in the ANC, which were revitalized by the contemporaneous success of Algeria's anticolonial battle against the French, and the Cuban revolution. He was part of an underground network of ANC's external mission, sent abroad to attain whatever training necessary—ideological or military—to seize the country by armed confrontation. This is what Kgositsile took with him into exile, a voracious resolve to return with the fury of millions. But as he so eloquently put it, for him "Armed struggle / Is an act of love" ("Red Song"); any violence not guided by discipline and commitment to the dreams of the collective was criminal. Therefore organizing and acting under clear objectives was central to his modus operandi; there is no such a thing as revolutionary soloist. His involvement in the Black Power and Black Arts Movements pivoted anti-apartheid, anticolonial, and American civil rights along the same axis of freedom dreams, as articulated in his poetry. Reading *Spirits Unchained*, his debut collection of 1969, is akin to being placed at the center of a Black universe around which orbits key political figures, including Frantz Fanon, Nelson Mandela, Nina Simone, Patrice Lumumba, and Lindsay Barrett. The collection maps a new world with centers of political production and resistance, relational identities unified by the same desires and by a common enemy, new social relations, and new grounds that reconfigured space and time as simultaneously fluid and contracted. That world was sounded by a new language drawn from Tswana oral traditions woven with African American parlance and vernaculars, and shaped by jazz and blues. Love is always the message, and the message is armed struggle. For Rap Brown he sings a praise song:

> Are you not the searchlight
> in our eyes red with the dust
> from the slave's empty grave
>
> . . .
>
> Some say it's youthful
> adventure in the summertime
> for they have lost natural instinct
> which teaches a man to be free
> ("WHEN BROWN IS BLACK")

Rap Brown was the leader of the Student Nonviolent Coordinating Committee (SNCC, pronounced "snik"), later changed to Student National Coordinating Committee to reflect its monumental shift away from nonviolence. Rap Brown was known to motivate and is famous for his observation that "violence was as American as cherry pie." His radical approaches to Black Power politics, which according to Kgositsile were not radical but man's "natural instinct" to attain freedom, are tied to the riots during the "long hot summer" of 1967, when revolts ensued in cities across America, having built up since the assassination of Malcolm X, and finally exploded, in the words of Langston Hughes in his prophetic "Harlem," with the assassination of Martin Luther King Jr. As seen in the refrain of Kgositsile's poem, Rap Brown would address the crowd, "What does a penny buy?" to which they would reply, "A box of matches."[5] Kgositsile aligned with this firebrand. This uncompromising reverence for revolutionary violence is what the CIA sought to subdue when in 1962 they, under the guise of a scholarship through their Information Agency, extracted Kgositsile out of the political hub of Dar es Salaam to place him in rural Pennsylvania, a school famous for its African alumni Kwame Nkrumah and Nnamdi Azikiwe. As it later transpired, they had envisioned isolating him from radical politics and, as with many such efforts among African intellectuals, inculcating the values and ideas of the United States in him. What a spectacular oversight on their part.

The oral traditions that informed Kgositsile's politics were couched in songs that functioned as vehicles to rally the broad community. These songs were a transmutation of practices that have historically expressed without compromise the total humanity of African people. The lyrics addressed urgent social issues—for example, bus boycotts, forced removals, and stay-aways. Music was, at an artistic level, the most advanced cultural affirmation of the people's determination to live in spite of the conditions with which they were faced. Through the evolution of song from *marabi* of the Johannesburg slums, to the penny whistle, workers' songs in the mines, to *mbaqanga* (a tenor of jazz with a South African accent), a mobilization of Blacks against the ruling class policy of oppression was fostered. The culture of resistance has always been contemporaneous with the political developments: continuous creativity and improvisation affirmed the lives of the oppressed as creative force. These songs were composed and sung at the same time, on the go. They are the fertile grounds of creativity out of which a distinct South African jazz was born. Groups such as the African Jazz Pioneers, the Jazz Maniacs, the Huddleston Jazz Band, and the Harlem Swingsters asserted an acoustic regime within apartheid's limiting parameters. Eminent cultural critic Lewis Nkosi would go on to dub this period the "fabulous decade" in capturing that Johannesburg-based Black modernity in full swing, informed by a multiplicity of cultural contexts, including jazz and literatures of the Harlem Renaissance.

Kgositsile carried this cultural archive with him into exile. He spoke to Black America in Setswana and mbaqanga, interweaving it with their African American vernaculars and blues. His staccato and percussive performances evoked bebop, and enriched vernaculars of jazz and Black arts poetry with a 1950s southern cosmopolitanism made up of cultures, languages, and sociopolitical orientations from Lilongwe, Lusaka, Lourenço Marques (Maputo), Bulawayo, Dar es Salaam, Harlem, and Salisbury (Harare), all constituting the cauldron of Johannesburg Black modernism at the time. His radical politics brought into powerful synthesis a geopolitical and transnational struggle against white supremacy and Western imperialism. In Black America, he adopted blues, bebop, and jazz as expressive of continuity with Tswana folk song, proverbs, and urban cultural expressions. He was a master at speaking to the collective using a language that invokes the collective's cultural values and self-image for purposes of spiritual cohesion and solidarity. In this sense, his poetry published in the States can be compared to that of Langston Hughes, who became enthused with blues and Black music and adapted blues verse as a basic stanzaic block to imprint on his verse the authenticity of the Harlem streets. Hughes's imagination as an artist reflected his commitment to the people of Harlem and their history, culture, and struggles. Black music was, for Kgositsile, the strongest art form to capture the African community and its spirit.

The vibrant musical suite in his fourth collection, *The Present Is a Dangerous Place to Live*, dedicated to Billie Holiday, Art Blakey and the Jazz Messengers, B. B. King, John Coltrane, Pharoah Sanders, and Hugh Masekela, reverberates in the archive and sounds out the indelible imprint he left on not only the African American literary scene but also its musical production. The poem "Pro/Creation," dedicated to Pharoah Sanders, emerged out of his friendship with Sanders and his South African wife, Thembi, and is expressive of how music had been deployed for purposes of pan-African solidarity throughout the long twentieth century to the contemporary moment. The poem was used by Sanders in the liner notes to his 1971 magisterial album *Thembi* and concretizes the relationship of conviviality between Black South Africans and Black Americans at the time. Musicians such as Don Cherry and Johnny Dyani recorded albums together, as did Sathima Bea Benjamin and Duke Ellington. How can we forget Nina Simone informing us that Miriam Makeba taught her the song "Westwind" during Simone's live recording of that song? This attests to the constellation of cultural influences, collaborations, exchanges, and inspirations that was fostered by South Africans in exile in Black America. Within this cultural matrix, which Henry Louis Gates Jr. would call a "blues matrix," artists who sought to affect an imaginative committed vision of social change looked to Kgositsile's clarity of vision with respect to politics and social transformation.

That members of the poetry outfit and purported grandfathers of the rap genre, the Last Poets, searched through the Black Arts Movement's bible—*Black Fire: An Anthology of Afro-American Writing* (1968)—for a name and decided upon Kgositsile's poem "Towards a Walk in the Sun" to achieve this goal is revealing of the stature of his work within that turbulent period. In a milieu when African Americans took on African names to redefine their identities (Leroi Jones became Amiri Baraka, and Paulette Williams became Ntozake Shange) against white America's ontological negation, Kgositsile represented that continent materially. Let us put the matter of their exchange to rest, since it has of late become a contested legacy.[6] The words "The Last Poets" do not appear in Kgositsile's poem "Towards a Walk in the Sun" that incited them. In the poem Kgositsile calls for the end of poetry and the beginning of armed confrontation, and David Nelson responds, "Therefore we are the last poets of the world." It is a practice of antiphony—call and response—without which the tradition of the Black expressive continuum from Africa to the diaspora would not be so reverberant. It is a powerful dialogue between two worlds where "Africa Speaks, America Answers," argued masterfully by Robin D. G. Kelley, out of which a new mode of expression was birthed. The Last Poets did not only respond to Kgositsile by name but considered his firebrand poetic as an archive from the motherland, to be mined for heightening consciousness in Black America. And that they did! Their cultural heirs Public Enemy, A Tribe Called Quest, and later Common and Dead Prez adapted their incendiary and politically charged poetry as a tool of mass conscientization. The role of exiled South Africans in the production of an African American Black modernity of the twentieth century should be taken seriously to disrupt the current reading of the two countries' relationship as a one way, north-to-south flow of influence. If the Last Poets were "Rap's Radical First Act," then what does that make Kgositsile?

The incisive role Kgositsile played as an academic during the tail end of the civil rights and Black Power era cannot go without mention. He, together with Dennis Brutus, conceived and installed the African Literature Association conference, which continues today as an institution par excellence of those literatures. He was a key interlocutor in formations of African studies programs in universities. When Black poets enjoyed appointment as writers-in-residence at academic institutions, he was one of the first to take up a post at North Carolina Agricultural and Technical State University. Further, when universities in the South sought to transform the humanities, they appointed him as advisor at Tulane University in New Orleans. He also edited a volume of African poetry, *The Word Is Here* (1973), which was used widely in emerging curricula to broaden the scope of understanding Black poetry. Through these efforts, Gwendolyn Brooks formally inaugurated Kgositsile as a permanent feature in the family album of the Black arts era. In her *Family Pictures* (1970) Brooks included three poems dedicated to "Young Heroes," Kgositsile being one of them. "Young Heroes: Keorapetse Kgositsile (Willie)" became the introduction to *My Name Is Afrika*. The three-part poem "Young Heroes" was reprinted in another Black arts seminal anthology, *The Black Poets* (1971), edited by Dudley Randall. Brooks highly recommended Kgositsile's poetry for the anthology *The Poetry of Black America: Anthology of the 20th Century* (1973), introduced by Brooks. In her introduction she writes, "Many applauders of black poetry have never heard of . . . the carefully rich technics of Audre Lorde and Keorapetse W. Kgositsile."[7] Brooks, Kgositsile, Randall, and Haki Madibhuti (formerly Don Lee, owner of Third World Press, which published Kgositsile's second collection, *For Melba*) collaborated as co-authors of the book *A Capsule Course in Black Poetry Writing*, published by Broadside Press in 1975. These seminal publications were central to transforming the curriculum of universities at the epicenter of budding African studies programs in universities across the States.

Kgositsile's departure from the States in 1975 was a timely one, buoyed by the arrival of a South African writer. In 1974 he had welcomed the young writer Mongane Serote to New York City, where Serote had arrived to study for his masters in fine arts at Kgositsile's alma mater Columbia University. The relationship between the two writers was mutually beneficial: Kgositsile was tasked with supervising Serote's dissertation in a formal capacity as professor, which resulted in Serote's *Behold Mama, Flowers*. On the other hand, Serote brought news of the incendiary developments within the country, the rising Black consciousness movements, and various facets of students-led organizations such as Black People's Convention and the cultural group Music, Drama, Arts, and Literature, of which Serote had been a member. Coming from a South Africa characterized by cultural blackout, where its older generations of writers had been banned, Serote devoured Kgositsile's work fervently. In *Behold Mama, Flowers*, we observe an active engagement with Kgositsile's fifth collection, *Places and Bloodstains*, as well as a wider consciousness of the Black world introduced to Serote through chasing jazz shows across state lines. In turn, Kgositsile's fifth collection took a turn toward his native country. Whereas his previous work had been dedicated to cultural and political figures of the Black diaspora, the poems in *Places and Bloodstains* are odes to mostly South African writers. The entire collection is "dedicated to the brothers and sisters who picked up arms to create a place for us in southern Africa," with poems for Can Themba, Ilva Mackay, Dennis Brutus, Es'kia Mphahlele, Gwigwi Mrwebi, Cecil Abrahams, Montshiwa Moroke, Zakes Mokae, and two poems for Serote. Their friendship and camaraderie forged in the United States were subsequently expressed through their literary offerings: Serote's 1981 novel, *To Every Birth Its Blood*, takes the title from Kgositsile's poem "My Name Is Afrika," and Kgositsile's penultimate collection, *This Way I Salute You*, gleans the title from Serote's poem "City Johannesburg." That Serote became the third national poet laureate after Kgositsile's tenure as the second is testament to the roles they played in literature as a tool for social transformation and revolution.

Kgositsile's departure from the United States in 1975 was timely in many ways: the dissolution of the Black Power and Black Arts Movements is recorded as 1975, while on the other side of the Atlantic, the Soweto students' uprising in 1976 signaled a second wave of young South Africans that went into exile en masse. His departure from the States to Tanzania positioned Kgositsile to receive those students in East Africa. As an unwavering believer of direct-action protest and armed confrontation, Kgositsile extolled their unbridled courage and formidable spirit of resistance. The events of June 16, 1976, in turn bolstered Kgositsile's determination as a returnee of the first wave of exiles and transformed his vision of politics and his role in it as a writer. His post-U.S. poetry took a dialogic turn, transitioning into unapologetically partisan manifestos and positioning itself as a solid voice that concretized the dreams of the people, located within a liberation party committed to make those dreams a reality. As it were, receiving a pride of "young lions" from the

South African interior shifted the ANC's mission into the next phase of their tactical strategies, strengthening their forces to soon be "homewardbound." The poem "June 16 Year of the Spear" celebrates the youth and is brimming with exuberance in its expression of hope for a new day:

Freedomchild homewardbound
With an AK47 resting easy in my arms
. . .
I am June 16
I am Solomon Mahlangu
I am the new chapter
I am the way forward from Soweto 1976
I am poetry flowering with an AK47
All over this land of mine

While stationed at the University of Dar es Salaam, he was closer to Morogoro, 170 kilometers outside of the capital, where Julius Nyerere had apportioned land for the ANC to set up camp. Here the Solomon Mahlangu Freedom College (SOMAFCO) was set up to educate the post-1976 youth, some of whom Kgositsile led as part of the ANC delegation to the Second World Black and African Festival of Arts and Culture hosted in Lagos, Nigeria, in 1977. The students staged reenactments of the confrontation with the apartheid security police, disarming the local national army who were in attendance and who reportedly wept unreservedly. In a decisive moment for the liberation movement's relationship with culture as a weapon of resistance, the ANC's Mayibuye cultural ensemble, later Amandla cultural ensemble, became a core component of ANC's activities, spearheaded by Kgositsile. Years later he would be heartened to meet these students-turned-comrades in South Africa, who recited his work to him imitating his iambic voice. Till the very end he sustained this relationship with the youth and younger writers in democratic South Africa, providing indispensable mentorship that encouraged many who struggled to find their voices. His mission as a poet of the revolution was always informed by the collective.

It is not possible to offer well-rounded readings of his work published post–United States without the framework of the Cold War. Moving within the networks fostered by the ANC and its alliance, the South African Communist Party (SACP), and Mkhonto we Sizwe (MK), his circuit of engagements constituted close relations with SACP giants Moses Kotane, Duma Nokwe, J. B. Marks, and Alex La Guma (whom Kgositsile invited from Cuba to University of Dar es Salaam as writer-in-residence); while the geopolitics of ANC's relationship with the Soviet Union diverted his movements to Russia, Scandinavia, Cuba, German Democratic Republic, China, and the larger Soviet region. His work within the ranks of the Afro-Asian Writers' Association reflects these diplomatic relations and resulted in his poetry being translated into a plethora of languages, including Polish, Arabic, Russian, German, Mandarin, and French. His sixth collection, *Heartprints: Poems*, or *Herzspuren: Gedichte*, was published in Germany in a bilingual format in 1980. It was conceived as a tool for fundraising to keep the ANC's quarterly magazine, *Voices of Women*, in production. The ANC's, SACP's, and MK's transnational solidarities fostered within the continent, and particularly in southern Africa, inspired a turn to Kgositsile's self-identification as a poet of the revolution. He aligned his work with poet of Mozambican revolution Jorge Rebelo of Frente de Libertação de Moçambique (Liberation Front of Mozambique) and poet-president of the Popular Movement for the Liberation of Angola (MPLA) Agostinho Neto, citing their seminal work that infused their people's respective armies with the voices of the collective. They embodied Kgositsile's freedom dreams. His would become a key addition to the growing constellation of these liberation voices in the third world firmament, which illuminates and is illuminated by the work of Ho Chi Minh, Pablo Neruda, and Nancy Morejón.

It is also a body of work whose tenderness is palpable and reflective of how radical empathy can and must be a tool of revolution. The poems written for his first wife, Melba Johnson (published in his second collection of 1970, *For Melba*), daughters, mother, grandmother, and his sister-in-struggle Kate Molale, as well as those written in the moments of reunion with his sisters— Thuli, Dineo, Tshidi—in the 1980s in Botswana, flow seamlessly with a deep commitment to love, foster community, learn, teach, and grow even in the face of regimes that were determined to thwart any form of livelihood. His *When the Clouds Clear* (1990) is a rich-woven tapestry made from strands of communities, their respective dreams, the crushing weight of their expectations, personal triumphs and failures that are inevitably political, and inspiring hope to reinvent: a song of constant beginnings. Deeming himself "Manboy," he professes,

> Sometimes the childhood possesses
> And with ease carries heavy files of memory
> Which open without a creak
> Frightening me with knowledge I must now
> reclaim

The memory of his grandmother Madikeledi and his mother, Galekgobe, whom he christens "confidant," "trustee," and "ally," is a powerful and ever-present part of his identity, which we observe in the poetry, that commands and validates his desire for a decolonized South Africa. We observe the tropes of memory and desire in his exilic poetry in the interstices of temporal and spatial interrelated categories, between South Africa and the world, Indigenous knowledge systems and colonial epistemologies, politics and culture, poetry and music. Kgositsile's poems remained deeply committed to the contemporary moment, and in most instances, this is where the voice of the collective resides, their aesthetics, worldviews, songs, cosmologies, and interrelational subjectivities. Here, the collective song of resistance in South Africa merged into a chorus with the song of the diaspora and the working class in the global south. In his poetry, Sharpeville is resounded in Watts, California, and Soweto in Harlem; and Ornette Coleman's horn or Mongo's conga drums invoke the griots and dream keepers of yesteryear buried in Mafikeng. This is how "distances separate bodies not people." Finally, this spatiotemporal conflation and rearrangement underpins his devastatingly resolute "Requiem for My Mother":

> As for me
> . . .
> The roads to you
> Lead from any place
> I am.

This is a voice emerging from a depth of feeling located in that zone. The vision is always instructed by memory, and it is this living past that entangled his vision for a post-apartheid South Africa with that of the collective, the restoration of pride and dignity to the people and their cultures. This desire became compromised in the long battle post the release of political prisoners in 1990 and the long and fraught negotiations that took place between then and the first democratic elections held in 1994. To Kgositsile, the decades-long revolution that sent him into exile was not progressing to its logical conclusion of an armed confrontation, and the socialist dreams nourished by his comrades were collapsing before his very eyes, in tandem with the Berlin Wall and the Soviet Union. It soon turned into a long and drawn-out nightmare during the negotiations period between 1991 and 1993, and Kgositsile responded to the still-born revolution with his 1995 collection, *To the Bitter End*. The collection's title carries his resolve in its inner sleeve, "COME THUNDER! CONFLAGRA-TION! [. . .] I will tell you right here and now that, like Castro, no force on this planet can move me from conviction about the principles of socialism. To the bitter end. Socialism or death. *Daar's kak in die land.*"

While he returned to South Africa in 1991 to promote his seventh collection, *When the Clouds Clear*, the first to be published within South Africa by the Congress of South African Writers, Kgositsile was profoundly disillusioned by the dialogue of negotiation and decided to return to the United States. He taught at Denver University, and eventually moved to take up a post at the University of California in Los Angeles and spent the next six years following a pattern of spending six months in Los Angeles, where he taught one semester a year, and another six months at Fort Hare University in South Africa, where he taught the other semester. He finally returned and settled in South Africa in 2001. He published a selection of poems from previous publications in his *If I Could Sing* (2002) and *This Way I Salute You* (2004). He served as special adviser to ministers of arts and culture Pallo Jordan, Lulu Xingwana, and Paul Mashatile. In 2006 Kgositsile was inaugurated as second national poet laureate of South Africa, after Mazisi Kunene's tenure, which ended in 2005. In his speech, Jordan praised Kgositsile for being not only a truly engaged poet but also a political activist of long standing, "who like Mao Zedong and Pablo Neruda had mastered the art of producing politically inspired poetry that did not compromise poetics to make a political statement." He was honored with the degree doctor of literature and philosophy by the University of South Africa in 2012. He spent his time as a national ambassador of culture, outspoken critic of the "new" ANC, and a fervent cultural worker committed to mentoring a new generation of young South African writers.

On January 3, 2018, the year that would have marked his eightieth birthday, Kgositsile departed for the land of his ancestors. He had been working to complete his selected works published in South Africa under the title *Homesoil in My Blood* (2018). This posthumous collected works that you hold in your hands is a gift that seeks to encompass his long and fruitful journey as a global political and cultural figure committed to justice, inclusivity, and equality, to the very end. Here, sit and feast on these words, plunge into their depth of feeling, journey through their difficult yet poetic explorations of the human spirit, witness their anguish, let them spur you to action, and live in the legacy of their prophetic vision.

NOTES

1. Charles H. Rowell, "'With Boodstains to Testify': An Interview with Keorapetse Kgositsile," *Callaloo*, no. 2 (February 1978): 23.
2. Keorapetse Kgositsile, "Culture and Liberation in South Africa," *Lotus* (January–March 1978): 15.
3. Her memoir, *117 Days* (1965), is a recollection of this time. The Ninety-Day Detention Act meant one would be arrested for ninety days without trial or access to a lawyer; later doubled to180 days.
4. *Drum* was a magazine in 1950s South Africa, and writers and artists from that era are called the *Drum* generation or artists.
5. Keorapetse Kgositsile, interview with author, 2013.
6. See Walton Muyumba, "Rap's Radical First Act," *New York Times*, November 30, 2018, https://www.nytimes.com/2018/11/30/books/review/christine-otten-last-poets.html#click=https://t.co/PKLBHhSZ6b.
7. Gwendolyn Brooks, introduction to *The Poetry of Black America: Anthology of the 20th Century*, ed. A. Adoff (New York: Harper & Row, 1973), xxx.

KEORAPETSE KGOSITSILE

Spirits Unchained
1969

To the memory of

Bobby Hutton

and

Dedan Kimathi

To Gloria

We gave up laughter
Blindfold between the pages
Left right left right
We rehearsed our death

But the melody of memory
Lingered strained by bloodstained
Diamond, whiplash
And mother turned shadow

Now look at those eyes
Leaping from ghetto gutter
To godlike height
Reclaiming the childhood

For LeRoi Jones, April, 1965

Because finally things have come to this
White world gray grim cold turning me into a killer
Because I love love
Puerto Ricans and Black captive people piss
In the hallways and project elevators
This is the white face they vomit on
Not knowing but feeling the truth

Watchout,
There comes the Blackman!

In your airconditioned grotesque monstrosities
I cannot breathe
Your cold bricks are made of the pulp of my bones
The water my sweat and blood

All the machinegun happy verwoerds and johnsons
All the housewives at pta coldwar meetings
All the butcher criminals who sat in judgement
Over Lumumba, Mandela, Sobukwe, Brother Malcolm
All the infernal priests teaching Blackmen
Never to know the truth
All the apologists for obscene hatred
And domination by white faggots
All these ghosts are dying
I discovered the truth one more time

Watchout,
Here comes the Blackman!

    Can you do the dog?
    Did you ever drink skokian?
    Is Harlem a vice-infested nigger ghetto
    Or a house of truth?
    Is that Christ I saw in your bedroom?
    Are you looking forward to
    THE DESTRUCTION OF AMERICA,
    A concrete act by LeRoi Jones?

Watchout,
Here comes the Blackman!
He has seen the truth
He beats his drums without embarrassment
Swinging to the rhythm of his birth pangs

When Brown Is Black

(For Rap Brown)

Are you not the light
that does not flicker
when murderers threaten summertime
passions of our time
Are you not the searchlight
in our eyes red with the dust
from the slave's empty grave
sending chills through
lynching johnsons around the world
as their obscene ghettos
go up in summertime flames

Some say it's youthful
adventure in the summertime
for they have lost natural instinct
which teaches a man to be free

"What does a penny buy?"

Are you not the fist
which articulates the passion
of the collective power of our rebirth
Are you not the fist
of the laughter of the rhythms
of the flames of our memory

"What does a penny buy?"

The naked head of the fuse
is up in the air pregnant

with the flaming children of our time
when Brown is Black
blowing up white myths
which built up layers of mists
which veiled the roads to the strength
of our laughter in the sun

But some
eating their balls in empty statements
say: it is youthful
adventure in the summertime

Now we said
the game is over, didn't we?
when we reach the end of the line
the shit goes up in flames, don't I say?

"What does a penny buy?"

For Malcolm,
for the brothers in Robben Island
for every drop of Black blood
    from every white whip
    from every white gun and bomb
for us and again for us
we shall burn
and beat the drum
resounding the bloodsong
from Sharpeville to Watts
and all points white of the memory
when the white game is over
and we dance to our bloodsong
without fear nor bales
of tinted cotton over our eye

Go on, brother, say it. Talk
the talk slaves are afraid to live

"What does a penny buy?"
When Brown is Black

Brother Malcolm's Echo

Translated furies ring
on the page not thoughts
about life
but what should be
real people and things
loving love
this is real
the human Spirit moves
what should be
grinning molotov cocktails
replenishing the fire
WATTS happening
SHARPEVILLE burning
much too damn talking
is not
what's happening

Mandela's Sermon

Blessed are the dehumanized
For they have nothing to lose
But their patience.

False gods killed the poet in me. Now
I dig graves
With artistic precision.

Elegy for David Diop

He who thinks immortality
Flaming with furious fidelity
Could be dead has no head
You are the indignant air
Carrying fruit to nourish the continent
Unrelenting throbbing of the continent's heart
You are the dance and the dancer
The concrete foundation and the builder
Moving at lightning speed
Mating with fertile future
Refusing the touch of the stench
Of the carcass of rancid europe
I saw you explode
In Sharpeville burning
In Watts and the paddies
Of Vietnam and all dawn
Long I, the desert palm
Drinking from your spring

Danced to the elegant
Replenishing of your majestic fire
Roaming the rhythms of your eternity
Because you are not a man
You are what Man should be
Eternal like the Word

Ivory Masks in Orbit

(*For Nina Simone*)

these new night
babies flying on ivory wings
dig the beginning

do you love me!

son gawdamn
i saw the sun
rise at the midnight hour

300 sounds burn
on the ivory bespeaking
a new kind of air massive
as future memory

this like a finger moves
over 300 mississippis
rock the village
gate with future memory
of this moment's riff

the sun smiles of new
dawn mating with this
burning moment for the memory
can no longer kneel-in

do you love me!

88 times over lovely
ebony lady swims in this
cloud like the crocodile
in the limpopo midnight
hour even here speaking
of love armed with future
memory: desire become memory
i know how you be tonight!

Lumumba Section

Searching past what we see and hear
Seering past the pretensions of knowledge
We move to the meeting place,
The pulse of the beginning the end and the beginning
In the stillnesses of the night
We see the gaping wounds where
Those murderers butchered your flesh
As they butchered the flesh of our land
Spirit to spirit we hear you
Then blood on blood comes the pledge
Swift as image, in spirit and blood
The sons and daughters of our beginnings
Boldly move to post-white fearlessness

Their sharpnesses at the murderer's throat
Carving your song on the face of the earth
In the stillnesses of the night
Informed by the rhythm of your spirit
We hear the song of warriors
And rejoice to find fire in our hands
"Aint no mountain high enough . . ." Dig it,
The silences of the wind know it too
"Aint no valley low enough . . ."
Freedom, how do you do!

Spirits Unchained

(*For Brother Max Stanford*)

Rhythm it is we
walk to against the evil
of monsters that try to kill the Spirit
It is the power of this song
that colors our every act
as we move from the oppressor-made gutter
Gut it is will move us from the gutter
It is the rhythm of guts
blood black, granite hard
and flowing like the river or the mountains
It is the rhythm of unchained Spirit
will put fire in our hands
to blaze our way
to clarity to power
to the rebirth of real men

To Fanon

Tears,
hiding behind a doomed god
no longer define
the soul
because of your shock therapy
history's psychosis will be cured
once soft shack-born melodies explode
in love-loving hollers
in the womb of the future
exposing the shallow trenches
of make-belief history to the fury
of the midday sun
and now lovers weaving
their dreams into infinite
realities with ghetto charms will
with the light of the poet
show Jesus miracles

Song for Aimé Césaire

The fragrance of rebirth
is the rhythm of our movement
as I laugh
or jumpandlaugh
on time or stone
but I cannot lean on the groaning years
breathing on time
as wave rides on wave

as Detroit follows Newark
Setif Sharpeville
We revere you, Césaire
for now we know
icebergs can go up in flames
we know
we cannot lean on time
because in every corner of the memory
the years are groaning
for us to up and blaze
so I jump or laugh on time or stone
as my head spits flames
from Zimbabwe to Watts recreating
elegant memories of you

My Name Is Afrika

(*For Nqabeni Mthimkhulu*)

All things come to pass
When they do, if they do
All things come to their end
When they do, as they do
So will the day of the stench of oppression
Leaving nothing but the lingering
Taste of particles of hatred
Woven around the tropical sun
While in the belly of the night
Drums roll and peal a monumental song . . .
To every birth its blood
All things come to pass
When they do

We are the gods of our day and us
Panthers with claws of fire
And songs of love for the newly born
There will be ruins in Zimbabwe for real
Didn't Rap say,
They used to call it Detroit
And now they call it Destroyed!
To every birth its pain
All else is death or life

For Spellman at Spelman

For me, always
in the tapestry of the vision
of our song, the sounds begin
or continue as they will, always
   The young are no longer
young. Do not talk of suffering,
they say, the ocean knows the taste
of our blood. Do not talk of militancy;
all that is information
all that is useless, really,
unless it be our method
in formation. Leaders is what
we want, the young
say. A. B. lead us.
   The young are
no longer young, moving, as they do
from flesh to blood to spirit
on spirit and the pledge

I Am Music People

(For Lindsay Barrett)

Names, songs,
Places we only remember
In the blood like everpresent melodies . . .
Names like places are concrete like a song
Perhaps even deeper than the eye
For our images remember more than white whips
Malcolm, the mover and the moved,
Malik, a monumental name, strong thrusts
Of our movement as our fire
Like Trane, burns a concrete song . . .
Names give birth to people in places anytime
Lindsay,
It is a veritable song this song you sing
Full of blood and larger than desire
Keep singing, brother,
It is a cleansing this song
Showing us our 'flute and flame'
To give birth to a people
Singing our name concrete
As places and a song
Steeped in blood, the only
Gateway to our place under the sun

Origins

(For Melba)

deep in your cheeks
your specific laughter owns
all things south of the ghosts
we once were. straight ahead
the memory beckons from the future
You and I a tribe of colors
this song that dance
godlike rhythms to birth
footsteps of memory
the very soul aspires to. songs
of origins songs of constant beginnings
what is this thing called
love

For Melba
1970

And the Long Story

It was at the break of our day
And she-without-fear sang:
Burn their books. Burn
Their heroes. Burn . . .
Take a backward step in
A forward direction and burn
She says no longer will I sing:
They are gone, my children.
It was at the break of our day
And she said, the native voice from the future
I accept I accept I was raped
I was twisted about I was twisted around
I accept the fire from the future

Song for Melba

We grew then

And we said,
Evil and then pain of evil
Be trampled underfoot
To ashes and dust . . .

We grow

And the blood of the birth of laughter
Gives way to the face
Of the sons and daughters of our Sun

Till now in the stillnesses
    (But not silence to the lover's eye)
Of our determined motion
Like the wind, the face
Of our sons and daughters,
Born every day like the sun,
Moves on to their laughter
And the flow of their birth

And we grow

MMABATHO: Dakar, 1966

Till life or passion
do us part and now
this murmur squats
across the bare back
of my mind's home

in moments weaving
endless nights across
these shores while
the wave's elbow
kisses the air: you
are not a missing shadow

found by memory and desire
for the once-potential nightmare
wields the fragrance
of the odor of
the flesh of your soul

The Creator

you are the creator
fecundant monument
palpable breath
of the sun shining
even at the midnight hour
with the flesh of the soul
you create new gods
you shatter yesterday's
bleeding sufferings. the waters
of your eternal spring
drown today's debris
preparing for a naked
future. give me
your cosmic embrace
give me the essence
of this moment eternal
like the sky's horizon. you are
the creator of new gods
let me bask in the rhythm of your smile
tropical as tom-tom ecstasy

Indeed in Deed

Across continents on fire
Vampires fly against the wind
Do we lack specific answer?
Oceans of memory
Giantstep in upright path

The newborn infant asks which
Way is the way to the way
The unrelenting tide sticky
As mountains of wax
Giantsteps
To reclaim the childhood
We rebuild swallow-slow
But we rebuild
How deny specific deed is
Specific answer? SPEAK!

For Those Who Love & Care

Who does not get what
and how not
after the descent
into points further south
of the iceboxed heart
you emerge
with pangs of rebirth
the inevitable dissent
knowing
all the thens and whens
knowing
who gets what
and how
grinning excellent madness

True Blue

Do not be dis-spirited
Because
You can
Move the wall aside
       in
  the end
Even when you move to
The outskirts of your honor
Do not be dis-spirited
By the chains of dishonor
Keep on burning
Heaven can wait
Baby this is soultime!

Of Death and Lives

Some kind of hue
Blue and thick as a minute
To the midnight snakes death doses
Across desire though some,
Perhaps, do not know, this
Voice rips apart the night
Leaving silent evening bloodied
But every road leads some
Place even at the darkest hour . . .
Our passions now muddied haunt
The night with silent shrills only
The lover's eye can hear but

The finger of love moves on
Relentless as the voice of lightning
There will be no hesitation
For communion at dawn, your nipples
Salty with last night's stale
Tears waving into my lips
Searching for me in my breath

Death Doses

here i lie in bed looking
at my heart's bulldozed personal tyrannies
blood flows like a lazy river
out of my soul gored
by the poison blades of selfish morality
    loneliness is self-
    imposed shipwrecked desires
    on the stillness of the impartial sea
    the heart no longer listens to the wind
    the waves like
    aborted children
    die deserted by the wind
    the heart wanders lonely
    remembered pleasures afloat
    drifting on an endless voyage
    happiness, you petulant whore,
    who is going to be your man?

Death Doses No. 2

These days are so long
pain has wrenched me
down to the marrow
defying my brandied escapes
which were no escape

can you stand astride
your possible grave, teetering
like debris to the impartial sea?

is escape perhaps turmoil
concealed like the assassin's dagger–
perhaps just a fancy dream house
with no room for if but maybe perhaps!

this road is too narrow perhaps
for company other than alloyed ego
and fallen courage which disappears like
a mirage. If perhaps not, maybe just
listening to little heart steps reluctant
to follow from the fall

these days are so long
and I wonder, hating
all imprecise cowardice

Death Doses No. 3

Days like these are
a system of hell
you need more
than a poem for a cure
treasures of recorded feeling
like that I have been through
agony is old
as the creation of feeling
I say days like this
are a system of hell
my heart cannot dance here
hear the very air stick its poison finger
in the inner regions of the heart
being, as I am, from
everywhere I have been, I say
later for similar possibilities

My People When Nothing Moves

when nothing moves anywhere
the only motion is the noisy
stillness in me

should you then
            long for
                        me
look for
    me

        in forbidden songs
        searching in the light
        beyond petrified hypocrises

Come Duze

Can't go to meet The Man at early morning,
babes, because clear as the midday sun,
I'm going to meet myself . . . .

Once . . .
One time, you said
You made
A connection
Hear the rhythm here
Smile in your thigh
Friday
    No flights from real sights

Inevitable rebirths in
Soul confrontation. Dreams
Come home to roost
Friday, elegant
Like what and where,
You choose. You know
The sound is
Compatible ecstasy
Timeless at early morning
Friday
The rhythm smiled
In your thigh
And I made
A connection

3000 Miles Apart

'65, turbulent
storm: stale tears anguished
the hollow heart entangled
in the weed of memories
doomed to haunt the durance
here now breath to breath
breath broader than
breast of rain
hear our singular pulse
heedless of sham
leap sharp as brushfire

Of Us for Us

I know my name
which denies no mask
made obsolete by ghouls
and oxford pants
that covered no balls
my name wore the mask
to hide the cowardly tear
and I know my name
celebrating all time love hate
measured in broken chains
leaping in your stride
lighting oceans of fire
in your face without veil
nor shadow between my name and the tide

In Time

Can you be
desire or a movement
out of time a whisper
out of the eye: you are
my attitude this fire
the uncoiling cords of
a two-legged dream
rhythming my life in-
to an orgasm of eternities

By A. B. Inspired

    radiant monument of
    the black knight your
    heart wrapped in the
    ecstasy of a whisper
    opens like the sunflower

and though i don't have the joel blues
after and for him as a. b. sees
"if you hadn't heard me calling
i don't think i ever could been found
    it don't matter what i'm doing
    all i got to think about is you"

Tropics

Forever beginning
Forever laughing
And more laughter transpierced
By the birth of new eyes
Striding from petrified ice
To smoking stone to stone
Like bleeding memories
Of childbirth it is.
How deny that man can
Be born in the womb of a woman
Other than the overseas mother
Nursing his memories
Into upright method

Transpiercing western native township dooms?
They dubbed the township western
They did not know their irony
Here now beside the woman's face
Forever beginning
From ice to sunlit bush
Forever laughing

For Melba

Morning smiles
In your eye
Like a coy moment
Captured by an eternal
Noon and from yesterdays
I emerge naked
Like a Kimberley diamond
Full like Limpopo after rain
Singing your unnumbered charms

My Name Is Afrika
1971

To Hoyt W. Fuller,

Lele and Nti and The horse

The Air I Hear

The air, I hear,
froze to the sound
searching. And my memory
present and future tickles
the womb like the pulse
of this naked air
in the eye of a tear
drop. The dead cannot
remember even the memory
of death's laughter. But memory
defiant like the sound of pain
rides the wave at dawn
in the marrow of the desert
palm: stands looking still
and the bitter shape
of yesterdays weaves
timeless tomorrows
in the leaves
of laughter larger than
singular birth . . .

Impulse

. . . and the pulse of your mind
    flew,

    cold to the touch . . . you spit
        only excellent madness
        in the darkness of your pit
        make your own bed warm. The grave
        is not warm inside and
        your grave backbone like
        a gauge remained outside
        and your ghost walking like
        a dream laughing at your limp mind
            . . . "Merely
        coming into things by degrees"

Shotgun

Five deaths ago my
Name was born
Inside the thigh
Of a breath. Over

300 years in the grip
Of blood-drenched sweat I
Walk the flesh of the future
Like the heir's nimble
Grin at diamond dust. And my

Son playing in the nimble
Leaves of the mimosa soil-bound

Over 300 years . . . but every night
The red-lipped sun kisses the sea
The leaf mates even
With factory-filthed air
And love loves love
Bathed in a drop of the sun
Kissing the singing muscle
Of the mine laborer's son

Over 300 years of deballed grins . . .

Once-torture-twisted sighs
Of uprooted orgasms
Color the air with riffs
Of future pulse. Self-born
Maumau splits time's skull
With spearpoint flesh of mystic mask
Of built-in SHOTGUN weaved
In sounds like my daughter's
Memory of anguished joy in nigger-
Hard shadows screwing
The right moment . . . Uptight
The raggedy-ass prophet says
Everything is alright . . .

Mayibuye iAfrika

like the memories
of fatherless black children
become fathers of desire
in fox-holes before
they are old enough to build
cattle by the riverbank

the dancing road
uncoils in the ear
pierced by the finger
of the slender smile
of tight roots . . . these
retrieved eyes across the tight
belly of a pregnant drum
these are the words
of an ancient dancer of steel
—the children of a person
    share the head of a locus—
and who cannot say
life is
an unfolding proverb
woven around
the desire of the memory
of the belly dance

i remember
the taste of desire
crushed like the dream
of ghetto orphans rendered
speechless by the smell
of obsolete emasculation

but this morning
the sun wakes up
laughing with the sharp-edge
birth of retrieved root
nimble as dream
translated memory rides
past and future alike

Could Be

Vibrations in the womb I
Hear shake aplenty
While some memories slobber
On this moment's pulse, too

Lazy to remember. Perhaps
Just a strange breed of song,
But shake aplenty;
Even here in this stale

Air there is laughter.
My red-lipped son could
Be a wino drunk with
The condensed laughter of a distant

Drum, or a dancer,
Perhaps a way into things like
Memory could be just
A coil around time
Or many a slip between
The skin and the melody

Random Notes to My Son

Beware, my son, words
that carry the loudnesses
of blind desire also carry
the slime of illusion,
dripping like pus from the slave's battered
back. e.g. they speak of black power whose eyes
will not threaten the quick whitening of their own intent.
What days will you inherit?
What shadows inhabit your silences?

I have aspired to expression, all these years,
elegant past the most eloquent word. But here now our
tongue dries into maggots as we continue our slimy
death and grin. Except today it is fashionable to
scream of pride and beauty as though it were not
known that "Slaves and dead people have no beauty."

Confusion,
In me and around me,
Confusion. This pain was
Not from the past. This pain was
Not because we had failed
To understand:
THIS LAND IS MINE.
Confusion and borrowed fears
It was. We stood like shrubs
Shrivelled on this piece of earth
The ground parched and cracked.
Through the cracks, my cry:

And what shapes
In assent and ascent
Must people the eye of newborn
Determined desire, know
No frightened tear ever rolls on
To the elegance of fire. I have
Fallen with all the names I am
But the newborn eye, old as
Childbirth, must touch the day
That, speaking my language, will
Say, today we move, we move. . . .

To Mother

Toward the laughter we no longer
know; this way we must from now
on and always, past shapes
turned into shadows of wish
and want, regret too. Your
eye, I know, is stronger than faith in
some god who never spoke our language.

And there it seems to have been aborted.
Words, and they are old and impotent. Here
a slave will know no dance of laughter.

What of the act my eye demands
past any pretentious power of any word
I've known? My days have fallen

into nightmarish despair. I know
no days that move on toward laughter,
except in memory stale as our glory.
I see no touch of determined desire
past the impotence of militant rhetoric.
The anguished twists of our crippled day will not
claim my voice. Woman dancer-of-steel,
did you ever know that the articulate silence
of your eye possessed my breath for long days?
Yet still I know no dance but the slow
death of a dazed continent.
We claim the soil of our home
runs in our blood yet we run
around the world, the shit of others
drooling over our eye. We know
no dance in our blood now but doom.
So who are the newlyborn
who, unquestionable,
can claim the hands of the son?

My People No Longer Sing

Remember
    When my echo upsets
    The plastic windows of your mind
    And darkness invades its artificial light
    The pieces of your regrets hard to find
              Remember
    I shall only be a sighing memory then
    Until you look in the fiery womb of sunrise
    Retrieving songs almost aborted
    On once battered black lips
Remember
    When you get sickandtired
    Of being sick and tired
    To remind the living
    That the dead cannot remember

To a Black Woman, Insane

Insane ecstasy retaining my sanity,
Though full of fear, learned childlike.
Perhaps it is a badge of fallen courage?
Or is it of things yet to come? Perhaps
You should never open your eyes
Reflecting my wants so precisely,
As yours. Why people defy themselves
I wonder. How long is flight to insanity?

To My Daughter

There was a time
When I, too, thought eye
It was would take me
To the thrust of our intended purpose.
I did not know this illusion,
Responding, as I did, to word
With word.
        Did we think this was
The way to family, to protection?
But the peasant can still
Not stay until moonlight
In the paddy or the mealiefield.
Should you one day
See a man's back wobble to your eye
Like a scab or pus over all
The wounds you have known,
Tell your sister or brother,
Your father was once a dreamer.

Sift and Shift

(for ed spriggs & all my friends known & unknown to me)

When the image slips
through the fingers of our mind
like the passing wind
or meter and rhyme without substance
is it because there is nothing to hold?

Here we stand you and I
from coast to coast the tide
raging across continents and we
hear the unrelenting song
of the young talking drum:
"Sift and Shift"

When the image slips
and we do not
sift and shift
is it because
there is no blood of sacrifice?

O, selfish terror, you
fearful tyrant forever misleading us
by threat of pain in the flesh,
when is death death!

Here we stand you and I
and the unrelenting talking drum
and sift and shift we must
lest we like cowards
bear sons without memory
nor images to weave their song

Vector or Legacy

Some day soon, someday soon . . .
we forever say
and the children more rib than child
ribs clear as guitar strings to strike the bloodsong
their smiles butchered to death long
before they meander out of their mother's womb
keep glistening in the sun with sweat
of hopeless search for crumbs
any minute and every minute
they scramble for orange peel
from garbage pail or sometimes
a whole rotten banana from some
fat-bellied bastard's trash can
every minute and any minute they are here
swayed by hunger pang from garbage pail
to garbage pail defying death-by-malnutrition
they are here the unnourished ones
to nourish your desire
the pangs in fleshless rib
clearer than glib verse or song ask now
do you still say some day . . .

Bleached Callouses, Africa, 1966

Bleached sensibilities of the world
Did your eye ever cry
Blood tears or did
You choose pale frozen cud
For your heads. Dismayed

By dust you count
The clouds but the air
Stands still and some
Laughed but did not dismiss
This malady. The only
Motion is . . . But . . . heyi
Wena heyi . . . ! Do
You know not of power
Beyond proclamation? Oh yes,

I sit under the sea
And watch your perverted breath
Teetering before the glare of this motion
Parlez what? . . : your mama still
Chews kola muddy-eyed
She saw you move
Caucasus, almost carcass,
In the grip of indignant baobab
Her tear froze to your rancid breath
Quack magicians of the world
Don't you know don't you know
Even the roots of the dead baobab
Tree remain in the soil? Oh, weak-kneed
Dreams abandoned by hope slobbering
Fat-bellied in the mud do you ever

Have dreams with calloused hands
Do you ever see the tubercular
Shadow of your father numbed
By endless kneeling abandoning
Memory and desire choking
So that you can breathe

Where then where
Is the flesh of the rhythm
You preach. Your touch
Is blue-eyed rubber-stamped
FOR MASTER'S AMUSEMENT
But beware: listen
To the noisy stillness
Of the spearhead wind rhythm
Pulsations from thorny mimosa
To palm through art-
Ichoke to the naked bone of the baobab
Tree for, manchild, said the Tswana
Sage, marry your mother and
Bear yourself your own brothers
Because a thing don't mean
A thing if it don't move

The Lip Trick

Then ask any man,
is honesty passionate
foaming at the mouth
like an epileptic?
    These here must

be magicians. Hear
their wails "tear"
walls of snow down to smithereens,
their blood screams racing
through gullible ghetto gutters.
    But I cannot see the ice
melt before my very eyes.
This is
CHANGE?

The Nitty-Gritty

These in need
of once fearless songs
now frozen on battered black lips
recreated the music

Apostle Bird spread the message
floating high on his horn
He didn't want filthy blood on his hands

Lady Day spread the gospel with her voice
Is it because they knew what she was saying
That they killed her?

Lumumba of the Congo
didn't preach on the bongo
But they killed him also

I still hear them out loud
Lumumba, Lady Day, Bird

To those with ears to hear
They all said
FUCK ASSIMILATION
Get your values together!

And they in need
of once moving songs at once
started to recreate the music

Time

This moment
   like a tyrant strides
   across sunrise and sunset
   claiming its own
   panoramic view
no matter what the recorded lies

This moment
   like a tyrant strides
   across Meadowlands or
   Harlem streets painting
   tomorrows against today's
   fading moments of public hide and weep

And walks these
sidewalks with Ray Charles
Georgia on the mind
Is it not the right time!

New Dawn

(for afrika, asia, south & afroamerica)

"Integrate bloodpools not toiletrooms,"
Malik's song resounds
In my heart

Between the sun and the mountain top
The bride smiles and beckons
Her breath a lead perfume
Enchanting the hearts of real men

Up on the mountain
Lies the new dawn
Up on the mountain
The bride beckons impatient
Up on the mountain, my song
This is a rebirth

Inherent and Inherited Mistrusts

I woke up this morning,
Listened to their radio, read
Their papers, history books also.

Now can a spirit that sings
A new kind of god
Bond to the design
Of a shithead devil?

The shit hit imperialist fans in the Congo
Colonial nuns hit their front pages losing
Their papal virginity. Perhaps their pope foresaw
Their need for prophylactic supplies.
And they will say you are a racist when all
I learned at their schools was what not to be

    (Charlie, don't you know I'm going
    To stop singing "the man" blues!)

No more nightmares for me now
Only freedom on my mind
No more iffy concessions for me now
Only Lumumba incarnate in black children

    (Charlie, don't you know
    You're living on borrowed time?)

Symptoms

Lately there has been too
Damn talking much. But you
Wake up after night knowing
Your days have been no different.

On these bloodstained sidewalks
When grins of ghouls ask you
To forget the nature of these fiends
Brutal acts are quickly rudely remembered

There are whispers in your eye:
Damned are these criminals,
Their empire must
Die dry as a frigid whore

They whisper,
Those heads bashed open
Or mashed to a pulp,
Or scream, like

Your ancestor's genitals disembodied
For the amusement of some devil.
They whisper or scream. Still
We talk. And talk

Flirtation

Against these two
pillars and the evening
sun stands the baobab
as I stand
between memory and desire,
AFRIKA! the memory
that lingers across the hovering
womb of my desire at dawn.
AFRICA, the stench of absence
AFRIKA, the fragrance of rebirth

Conditioned

(or educated kaffir style)

Dreams, like disembodied
penises on perverted college
toilets walk these paved
sidewalks. Processed
echoes of papered hypocrisy
crumble in programmed fate.
But twisted or petrified,
this way or that, they wait,
without memory nor future,
they wait, so conditioned
they do not even despair

Innuendo

I heard voices
and anguished songs
in those days
i said listen
to the voices listen
to the cries of death
you laughed
at the pulse of my mind
in those days
we took time
to look at deeds

indeed we also saw viper's
eyes rasping through
the hole where your life used to be
in those days
when you laughed
we took time to remember

Axiomatic

Roots
long as ancestral ties
assert singular birth
burning
straight paths through
the womb of the earth
SCREAM NOW!
burning
pants off false guardian gods
scorching their iced phallus
like mbaula coal
black from the bowel
of the earth burning
red unrelenting like
the bitter smell of Sophiatown winters

Bandung Dance

This dancer defies fatigue
This dancer carries her fire,
Dancing with Shaka's battered spear

Up on the tree
That bears no fruit every morning
She nourishes her womb

But, young man,
Even you over there, do you
Know whose death her eye mourns?

For Afroamerica

when your days were made
of walls cold
and whiter
than natural death
when deranged vipers
sliced through your genitals
my body was one
huge bleeding ball.
Now
there will be no ifs
red-lipped dreams too
long deferred
explode
Now

truths
defiant like volcanoes emerge
taller than shadows
from ghetto magicians
Now
from the asshole of america
gutter smells rush
the blood like
a stampede to the head
scorching centuries-long tears
up and down the land

Now
I see
Patrice and Malcolm
in your step as you
dance near the sun
your hand outstretched
to embrace that long
deferred day so close
Now
I can see
ghetto smells going
up in smoke up and down
the land exploding in
the asshole of america
I can see that day
teasing like a whore, screaming,
NOW

No Celebration

But the day is not here yet to sing:
No more blues. No more stale tears
To claw some nigger's way to crumbs,
Slime dripping down the long-broken spine.

The day is not here yet to sing:
No more snow-crust blues when
The warrior leaps to act, eyes
Spitting fact of this moment
When our children and us turn
Adult, knowing,
The roots of the uprooted knowing
No more hesitation

In the Nude

Because
I wondered
In the maze
I wandered
And I saw god naked
In front of a mirror
With a microscope
Scrutinising the bleeding
In his acquired self
I said, Lawd,
What's happening?
Plastique in his hand

Tensed like an assassin
He said
    Ain't that a bitch!
Ain't that a bitch, he mused
And wandering
I wondered

Of Yesterday's Tomorrows

Never talk sterile old shit, he said.
He said, it don't make no sense,
The back of his mind bent,
Heavier than centuries I know. Then

Came my reply,
My song's boundary is beyond the twilight
The feet patter the rhythm
Weaving a new kind of dance
Awakening gods limp with slumber.

Epitaph

I was burying 300 groaning years
    And a Texas cowboy whitelipped,
        "We shall overcome!"

The pale imperialist moon was fading
    And I heard Verwoerd holler,
        "Keep the world white!"

We were rolling the coffin of imperialism
    to the colonial graveyard
And millions of Black people were dancing
    by the graveside
I was walking down bloodstained streets
    of Sophiatown and Harlem

And the beast gave me a rabid missionary grin

Don't you know he tried to buy my conscience
    with bloodstained bills
And adolescent fascist nuns carried their prophylactic
    supplies to the Congo!
I was listening to the wind
    And a voice thundered,

"Damned are they that ransacked the world!"
    And Black children laughed and danced
        To the rhythms of a new promise

Like the Tide: Cloudward

Turning here
Or returning there
A fractured rhythm from
The distant past makes demands

Or the image summoning
The existence of things
Or exploding the core of
The sinister rot our minds must vomit
When the cloudward flood screams
And some panting and fear-ridden
Wish to have been born without as
Much as a teaspoonful of brain
Soldiers or architects
We might have been. But here we stand torn
Between academic masturbation and splitting
Or chiselling words leaving the air unreddened
Where for humanity a little wrench
Would have sufficed for salvation. But
Words, be they elegant
As verse or song
Robust and piercing as sunshine
Or hideous memories of our
Cowardice in bondage are meaningless unless
They be the solid coil around our desire and method
Or the "most competent rememberer." May we

Turn here
Or return there
Where a fractured rhythm from
The distant past moves us

No Tears in the Tide

Do not cry wings
You are no flying machine
You can not cry wings
You are no vulture looking for prey
Sing wombs, life needs
A new mother. Sing wombs,
Bursting with specific life.
Weave a song with a movement
To celebrate the act you fathered.
Do not cry wings
There is nothing to run away from
But shadows of vampires in flight.
Better see the shape of things, says
The presence of my woman. Dig it? A spade
Is a slave is a spade, don't I say?

Towards a Walk in the Sun

THE WIND IS CARESSING
THE EVE OF A NEW DAWN
A DREAM: THE BIRTH OF
MEMORY

Who are we? Who
were we? Things cannot go on much as
before. All night long we shall laugh
behind Time's new masks. When the moment
hatches in Time's womb we shall not complain.

Where, oh where are
The men to matches
The fuse to burn the
Snow that freezes some
Wouldbe skyward desire

    You who swallowed your balls for a piece
    Of gold beautiful from afar but far from
    Beautiful because it is colored with
    The pus from your brother's callouses
    You who creep lower than a snake's belly
    Because you swallowed your conscience
    And sold your sister to soulless vipers
    You who bleached the womb of your daughter's
    Mind to bear pale-brained freaks
    You who bleached your son's genitals to

Slobber in the slime of missionary-eyed faggotry
You who hide behind the shadow of your master's
Institutionalized hypocrisy the knees of your
Soul numbed by endless kneeling to catch
The crumbs from your master's table before
You run to poison your own mother. You too
Deballed grin you who forever tell your masters
I have a glorious past; . . . I have rhythm;
. . . I have this; . . . I have that. . . .
Don't you know I know all your lies?
The only past I know is hunger unsatisfied
The only past I know is sweating in the sun
And a kick in the empty belly by your fatbellied master
    And rhythm don't fill a empty stomach

    Who are we? All night long
    I listen to the dream soaring

Like the tide. I yearn
To slit throats and color
The wave with the blood of the villain
To make a sacrifice to the gods. Yea,
There is pain in the coil around things

Where are we? The memory . . .
And all these years all these lies!
You too over there misplaced nightmare
Forever foaming at the mouth forever
Proclaiming your anger . . . a mere
Formality because your sight is colored
With snow. What does my hunger
Have to do with a gawdamm poem?

THE WIND YOU HEAR IS THE BIRTH OF MEMORY.
WHEN THE MOMENT HATCHES IN TIME'S WOMB
THERE WILL BE NO ART TALK. THE ONLY POEM
YOU WILL HEAR WILL BE THE SPEARPOINT PIVOTED
IN THE PUNCTURED MARROW OF THE VILLAIN; THE
TIMELESS NATIVE SON DANCING LIKE CRAZY TO
THE RETRIEVED RHYTHMS OF DESIRE FADING IN-
TO MEMORY

The Spearhead Wind Strides

History is still
a hair-raising slippery whore
though her skull be split.
Don't slip.
       At the hairsplitting
tip of time you stumble
macheting your path from here.
And though you heard Lumumba
and them are dead,
solid shadows spear their way
out of the clouds where
the spearhead wind strides
across your bare backbone
and on this splintered ice
on this debris from here,
and my song begins

The Gods Wrote

We are breath of drop of rain,
Grain of seasand in the wind
We are root of baobab,
Flesh of this soil,
Blood of Congo brush, elegant
As beast of dark cloud
Or milk flowing through the groaning years

We also know
Centuries with the taste
Of white shit down to the spine . . .

The choice is ours,
So is the life,
The music of our laughter reborn
Tyityimba or boogaloo, passion of
The sun-eyed gods of our blood
Laughs in the nighttime, in the daytime too
And across America, vicious cities
Clatter to the ground. Was it not
All written by the gods!
Turn the things! I said let
Them things roll to the rhythm of our movement
Don't you know this is a love supreme!
John Coltrane, John Coltrane, tell the ancestors
We listened, we heard your message
Tell them you gave us tracks to move,

Trane, and now we know
The choice is ours
So is the mind and the matches too
The choice is ours
So is the beginning
"We were not made eternally to weep"
The choice is ours
So is the need and the want too
The choice is ours
So is the vision of the day

The Long Reach

Need I say again
Where there is no clarity
There will be no depth
Only death.
          Touch the heart
And move. How old is the tree
Whose roots have defied death!

Are the people then on the move? Moved
By image that piles upon image
Sanctioned by the eye
Where the wind weaves this tapestry
In the song of tricontinental man

Are the people on the move?
Do you know then how
Old is the spirit
Whose roots are heart in the depths
Of Afrika; branches clasping the skies
In continents where the eye blazes   .
Like spear of gods!

The New Breed

(for don lee & mazisi kunene)

And generations still come or go
Mine, born deaf, never learned
The power of fire.
                    See how they run
Around the world on their knees!
Still you must wheel, bird of long reach
Move in the air with air
Out there. We are unleashed voices
And millions of hands to mold
What then is life, livable.

And breath is our hands
To caress breasts of fire
Which then is living, lovable,
Swing, blood of new breed, swing
Or do the dance of fire, thundering
In city or jungle with the newly born
Lancing whatever vein keeps poisoning
The body of the eye of your generation

For Eusi, Ayi Kwei & Gwen Brooks

In us and into us and ours
This movement rises every day
As the day whose fire informs
The rhythm of the sons who must live
After the death of those familiar faces

We move from origin,
The singular fruit, at times bitter
As the Sophiatown winters we did not create,
To roots, stronger than the grief
Which groans under the weighted
Centuries of systematic rape and ruin

We move from origin to roots.
Past the rancid face of anger and sorrow
Where I was a stranger to my breath
Rests the color of my eye
Calling my name
In the depths that reclaim
My pulse in the darknesses that alone
Remember the face of the warrior
Whose name knows a multiple doom
Before he is born to follow the eye
To the shapes remembered where the spirit moves
On to the darknesses the eye caresses
In us and into us and ours

Recreation

The face in my head
was born to tears, moaning
in silence to the grin acknowledging defeat,
to butchered smiles
and the anguish of a mother's tense womb

The face in my head
grows to the shape of a song,
remembering yesterdays without laughter
remembering more than I will ever
know between lips or time

What you hear between
the silences you are
witness to; the lover's
heart humming
the death of every thing but
acts of love; the steady hand
at the trigger moved
by the heart whose
blood has been a witness
to love, knowing that words
without the specific act to make
them concrete will hang frozen around
your face, to condemn you before
any breath or breadth of life
or love

To move towards
laughter has always been my desire
So here now knowing what
you should do you must do
right now, I laugh
moved by the memory
of hate and guns and love
moved by my son's memory
whose face is yet to be born
in the name of the act
triggered by us when we know
armed peace is an act of love
rhythm
    is
           this,
                  and clarity. The face
in my head remembering
more than I will ever know,
and the eye out there before
the hand, feeling the thens and
whys of yesterdays without laughter,
knowing the fire of today's how,
clasps the gun
that will set me free

Point of Departure: Fire Dance Fire Song

(A wise old man told me in Alabama;
"Yeah, Ah believes in nonviolence
alright. But de only way to stay
nonviolen' in dis man's country is
to keep a gun an' use it." Four
years earlier another wise old man
had told me the same thing near
Pietersburg in South Africa. He
said his words of wisdom is Sepedi.)

I. *The Elegance of Memory*

Distances separate bodies not people. Ask
Those who have known sadness or joy
The bone of feeling is pried open
By a song, the elegance
Of color a familiar smell, this
Flower of the approach of an evening . . .

All this is NOW

I used to wonder
Was her grave warm enough,
'Madikeledi, my grandmother,
As big-spirited as she was big-legged,
She would talk to me. She would . . .
How could I know her sadness then
Or who broke my father's back?
But now . . .

The elegance of memory,
Deeper than the grave
Where she went before I could
Know her sadness, is larger
Than the distance between
My country and I. Things more solid
Than the rocks with which those sinister
Thieves tried to break our back

I hear her now. And I wonder
Now does she know the strength of the fabric
She wove in my heart for us? . . . Her
Voice clearer now than then: Boykie,
Dont ever take any nonsense from *them*,
You hear!
              There are memories between us
Deeper than grief. There are
Feelings between us much stronger
Than the cold enemy machine that breaks
The back. Sister, there are places between us
Deeper than the ocean, no distances.
Pry your heart open, brother, mine too,
Learn to love the clear voice
The music in the memory pried
Open to the bone of feeling, no distances

II. *Lumumba Section*

Searching past what we see and hear
Seering past the pretensions of knowledge
We move to the meeting place,
The pulse of the beginning the end and the beginning
In the stillnesses of the night
We see the gaping wounds where
Those murderers butchered your flesh
As they butchered the flesh of our land
Spirit to spirit we hear you
Then blood on blood comes the pledge
Swift as image, in spirit and blood
The sons and daughters of our beginnings
Boldly move to post-white fearlessness
Their sharpnesses at the murderer's throat
Carving your song on the face of the earth
In the stillnesses of the night
Informed by the rhythm of your spirit
We hear the song of warriors
And rejoice to find fire in our hands
"Aint no mountain high enough . . ." Dig it,
The silences of the wind know it too
"Aint no valley low enough . . ."
Freedom, how do you do!

III. Fire Dance

There will be no dreaming about escape
There will be bullshit coldwar talk
    The fire burns to re-create
    the rhythms of our timeless acts
    This fire burns timeless in our
    time to destroy all nigger chains
    as real men and women emerge
    from the ruins of the rape by white greed

    The rape by savages who want to control
    us, memory, nature. Savages who even forge
    measures to try to control time. Dont you
    know time is not a succession of hours!
    Time is always NOW, dont you know!
    Listen to the drums. That there is a point of departure
    NOW is always the time. Praise be to Charlie Parker
    And it dont have nothing to do with hours

Now sing a song of NOW
A song of the union of pastandfuture
Sing a song of blood—The African miner, his body
Clattering to the ground with mine phthisis:
That there is murder. Do the dance of fire
The rhythm of young black men
Burning these evil white maniacs
Their greedy hands clattering to the ground
Like all their vile creations

Do our thing for the world, our world
NOW's the time, NOW's the time
A breath of love, song for my woman
Fire in her breast for our children
Supreme as a climax with the music of the wind
In her divine thigh there is life there is fire

IV. Spirits Unchained

(for brother max stanford)

Rhythm it is we
walk to against the evil
of monsters that try to kill the Spirit
It is the power of this song
that colors our every act
as we move from the oppressor-made gutter
Gut it is will move us from the gutter
It is the rhythm of guts
blood black, granite hard
and flowing like the river or the mountains
It is the rhythm of unchained Spirit
will put fire in our hands
to blaze our way
to clarity to power
to the rebirth of real men

For Sons of Sonless Fathers

Know you are a ghost
more pale than faded junk
lighter than snowflake
not even swayed
by song or dance from there
to here
not in jail no eyes
no ears no magic
you are the jail
ageless doom
ball of transparent pus where
the manhood used to be
son of a sonless father
yet you survive to die
and again die a death
unheralded by life
never been here nor there
how can I tell you to
remember the life of those ghouls
you envy is a death dance
without song nor natural laughter
memory you do not have
nor legs to stand or dance
so thinned
you are not even
your own possible shadow

Notes from No Sanctuary

1).

There are no sanctuaries
except in purposeful action;
I could say to my child,
There are wounds deeper
than flesh. Deeper and more
concrete than belief in some god
who would imprison your eye
in the sterile sky instead of
thrusting it on the piece of earth
you walk everyday and say,
Reclaim it.

But let it pass since
it is really about knowing today and how.
This is what it has come to. Daughters
and sons are born now and could ask,
you know: Knowing your impotence why
did you bring me here?

I could say:
Life is the unarguable referent.
What you know is merely a point
of departure. So let's move. But we have
been dead so long and *continue*. There will
be no songs this year. We no longer
sing. Except perhaps some hideous
gibberish like james brown making believe
he is american or beautiful or proud. Or
some fool's reference to allah who, like
jehovah, never gave a two-bit shit about niggers.

I could say, like Masekela,
We are in jail here. Which is
to say, We have done nothing.
I could say, . . . but see,
What difference does it make
as long as we eat white shit?
no matter what it is wrapped up in!

2).
How many deaths and specific
how or when ago was it
the rememberer said, where
to go is what to do?

   Still we talk *somuch*!

And cold black hustlers of my generation claw
their way into the whitenesses of their desire
and purpose. Here a slave's groan and shudder
is a commodity the hustler peddles newly-wrapped
in *brother, sister, revolution, power to the people* . . .

   So now having spoken our time or referent,
   a people's soul gangrened to impotence,
   all the obscene black&whitetogether kosher
   shit of mystified apes . . . Where then is
   the authentic song? The determined
   upagainstthewallmotherfucker act?

So say you say you float above
this menace, having violently tasted
white shit past the depths of any
word you know. Say you float above
the dollar-green eye of the hustler whose

purpose is cloaked in dashikis and glib
statements about revolution.

       Say you float
untouchably above this menace, does
your purpose, if there be one, propose
to be less impotent than this poem?

The Present Is a Dangerous Place to Live

1974, 1993

For all those brothers and sisters

Who struggled to look at the present

Straight in its dangerous face

And faced it in attempts to change it

And to the memory of:

Conrad Kent Rivers, Eric Dolphy, Henry Dumas

Whose still voices are out there

Hammered into an area of depthoffeeling

In the whirlwind with Coleman Hawkins

And Jean Toomer. They still reed and rite

Right here where they knew that "The Dixie Pike

Has grown from a goat path in Africa"

For Ipeleng

(*dedicated to Gerry T and the students who unleashed it at Bennett*)

I saw her come here with no words,
arms flailing air, past mother, thigh,
and blood. Here we begin again

We shall know each other
by the root of our appetite
or rhythm; Big Mama Juicy
Aneb seemed to say.
Her eye direct as comment. As
roaches or rats. As heads cracked
open for fun or lawandorder
in this strange place

When I woke up one morning
I saw her coming in the stillness
of her day and want. My eye sprung out
to embrace a season of dreams.
But she asked: if mother or father
is more than parent, is this my land
or merely soil to cover my bones?

The Present Is a DANGEROUS Place to Live

... One

I. In the Mourning

And at the door of the eye
is the still voice of the land.
My father before my father
knew the uses of fire
My father before my father,
with his multiple godhead,
sat on his circular stool
after the day was done. At times even
between the rednesses of two suns,
knowing that time was not born yesterday.
The circle continues
Time will always be
in spite of minutes that know no life.
Lives change in life
at times even rot
or be trampled underfoot
as the back of a slave.
There are cycles in the circle
I may even moan my deadness
or mourn your death,
in this sterile moment asking:
Where is the life we came to live?
Time will always be
Pastpresentfuture is always now
Where then is the life we came to live?

II. Beware of Dreams

The present is a dangerous place
to live. There were dreams once,
riding past and future alike; we
embraced the dream, drunk past
any look at the present in the face.
There were dreams once
and the illusion led
to the present.
There were dreams once,
gold, or red,/ green&black,
but the present is here
like me and you. And is articulate.
And knows no peace; neither do you
nor me if we are friends
enough to have known the dream

III. Without Shadow

I live here now
among my silences,
without life, an artifact
with as much use as a fart.

I live here now
silent. And the silence
does not have the peace
of understanding wrung from the past.

I live here now

without a shadow, but not even
dead since the dead are a vector
on the cycle of all that lives

Beware of dreams
they will so readily send
your eye shattering against nightmare
any time as any place you are alone.
You will moan your impotence or mourn
the quick rotting of the seed
that could have been your life,
silently. Now shuttered, you may run deep
enough into knowledge to understand this decay.
But your bony fingers remain so weak
they cannot seize even a moment.

IV. Mirrors, without Song

Do not tell me, my brother, to reach
out and touch my soul. My soul is
inside and thin
and knows your death too

Does it matter then how
often my teeth are seen
when I laugh less and less?

Morning does not wake up
with my eye out the window
moaning, or mourning,
a thing or day gone to waste

I die in the world
and live my deadness
in my head, laughing
less and less.
Do you see now
another day, like a slave,
shows its face to be nothing,
nothing but a mirror of the death of another?

When I laugh, my brother, less and less
do not tell me to reach
out and touch my soul. My
soul is inside and thin
and knows your death too.

Mystique

Even here we still dance
Though we don't do the soildance any more
The thread through and around our soul
We dance the deathdose
Where we don't have a toehold
We do the pusheachotheraroundandaway
Where we have forgotten the freedomdance
But the young are here
Even where the dance
Will not claim their memories
I have seen their eyes
Filled with the question:
Where is the warrior-prophet,
The carrier of our purpose?
Where is the collected step
The toehold of the coil
Through and around
Our soul and soil?

There Are No Sanctuaries except in Purposeful Action

... Two

I.

At the sound of the insane who think themselves sane
death's certain laughter eats away the vein of a whole
generation, leaving a legacy of spiritual and mental
bankruptcy, and decay, for the next. Violence, then,
documented past any argument by thousands of instant
deaths in terror-stricken township nights, is turned
inward. In piercing daylight too if you die you die.
We were so cool, we thought, shrouded in some shit
straight out of the pages of some american magazine

We die,
    our unthinking lives aborted by the heedless
    blade or bullet of a crazed thug. Or by a
    hasty police baton, boot or bullet

We die,
    quaffing shakespeare, the magna carta, the queen's
    language and sipping four o'clock tea

We die,
    though we remain animate in the silences that gaze
    at us through the cracks which scar millions
    of hollow and twisted township hearts

The fifties,
    the thick of all those whitenesses in our eye
    which seems to refuse to learn anything about power

The fifties,
    we are so bleached at our supposed hippest
    we call america home, edladleni

The fifties,
    but really any white time as any place
    where our Home is not our home

The fifties,
    we live in a madhouse

The fifties,
    this death is not knew

And days that pass me by will pass
With legs heavier than the slave's
Load. Presences shatter my sleep
With the strange brutality of the sun
On the back of a slave. Unable
To move, I shout,
GETOUTOFHERE, YOU HIDEOUS MOTHERFUCKA!

Because tomorrow should be a new day
Because tomorrow I should be older
I wonder if tomorrow I will be wiser

2. When Things Fall Apart

(after & for Chinua Achebe)

I lost my virginity and ran
into a world liced with whores

In the silences of the night,
often past the midnight hour,
when my voice dries up behind my tongue,
behind corpses that rattle in my mind
I wonder where the wind is

If you are afraid of your reflection
do not come my way
at times I am a mirror

If I am a receptacle
you will see your life
and the particles of your death
collected in me

There is no serenity here
past the slow rattle of our quick decay
lying 'in ambush around the street corners'

Mirror or receptacle where no dreams
come to roost in the night, I travel
from where we have been to where we might have been
Through the silences, my prayer:

Sound, where did even beer cans
find your relationship to the wind!
Spirit, I could dub you tree as baobab
but where did your soil go?

3. Exile

My memory is surrounded by blood.
My memory has its belt of corpses.
AIMÉ CÉSAIRE

And the ocean, my brother knows, is not our friend
I wonder if our ancestors might also be
in exile in places I dare not call by name

Where I sit among my silences,
where we yearn for a mood more ancient
than oceans, there is not community alarm

We try to begin again
but our dance is more waste
than the menstrual flow of a barren whore

"We are things of dry ours and the involuntary plan,
Grayed in, and gray." We bleed. We bleed.
Everywhere we walk are the white footprints
Our skeletons rattle under them

Did you say independence?
There are words here, we know, as any
place. Desire. And other appetites with the sharp
brutality of a blunt knife against a gumful of pus

When even your temper is sucked
for fun and profit like a whore's tit
I know we are pawns in a pimp culture

Lumumba, do you hear us?
I stand among my silences
in search of a song to lean on
but our breath lacks the rapid rhythm of the river

Is community more forgotten now than last
week's handshake? But the young are here.
They have ears. They will try to sing.
What songs will move them from our deadness?

4. Perception

(for gerry t & roger d)

Fire from stone on stone
to sound or magic
When night comes softly
the spirit is in ascent
her witness is music
warm touch early evening

Here is your ritual robe
here the grave of your dreams
stony cold and rusty
over there is the land of the rainbow
and other cities with their strange appetites

We search for the lost prayer
singing our magic song
to assemble the shattered pieces

5. Logistics

I saw her try to rise to sun
against pillars of ice slippery as pus
I saw her try to rise to song

womanchild, fragrance of rose and divine rage, rooted in
spirit fertile as my land now butchered by the devil's appetite;
they whose eye is glued to the devil's rectum, how can they
know there is more open between us than your thighs

night, like the color of our
desire, come bind us

but there are no distances here

even in the silence of the hotel room
whose fiction is too vicious for our dreams
night binds us like an oath

even against the hate and the hurt
of the vampire's teeth deep to our marrow
I taste the bone of our purpose
in the salt of your nipple
since the real man comes from his heart
I rise to offer you mine

where night binds us like an oath

. . . Three

Blues for Some Literary Friends & Myself

So now you walk the streets alone
at night. And your eye is not the coil
around your soul and soil

Your soul is soiled
Your memory is but a bloodstain
teetering on legs thinner than your shadow

Bwana poet please please tell me about love
or is yours tucked away too deep in the yellowing pages
of your books? Tell me about justice. About Amilcar Cabral.
Tell me about beauty. Or about the rhythm
of the sun, or the whip, on the back of a slave

Your soul is soiled
Your memory is but a bloodstain
And love is often just another word
for the boundary between soul and soul
and when you talked of justice did you know
that it is often just another word for compromise,
an affirmation of conflicting interests

O, fathers of my fathers and me
the voice of our land and blood is still
our skeletons rattle between the yellowing pages
and the young eyes will soon curse our cowardice
with a simple: What did you do between despair and desire

So now you walk the streets alone at night
If you are not an artifact dead as any curio,
Then like my sister said, sick of your loud mouth:

If you are the soldier they shout you are,
shoot! Shoot then. . . . shoot buckshot
in their hearts. Let them know that heaven
is a hole in the air and hell needs its
teeth kicked out, here and now!

Home Is Where
the Music Is

. . . Four

For Billie Holiday

Lady Day, Lady Day
Lady Day of no happy days
Who lives in a voice
Sagging with the pain
Where the monster's teeth
Are deep to our marrow

Lady Day of no happy days
Carried in a voice so blue
She could teach any sky
All about blues

Lady Day of no happy days
Mrs. Scag still roams
The treacherous ghetto streets
Of white design wasting
The youngbloods who think
Themselves too hip to learn
From your hurt.
                    Lady Day,
Them that got power,
Wealth and junk
Are still picking your pain
For profit and fun

Lady Day, Lady Day
Of no happy days
The willow still weeps for you
Though now we should know
That all tears are stale
Though now we should know
That tears aint never done nothing for nobody

For Art Blakey and the Jazz Messengers

For the sound we revere
we dub you art as continuum
as spirit as sound of depth
here to stay

       In my young years
I heard you bopping and weaving
messages I could only walk to
where wood mates with skin

I would have dubbed you godhead
but your sound rolled and pealed:
I am the drumhead even though
Blue Note don't care nothing
bout nothing but profit

How you sound is
who you are
where your ear
leans moaning or bopping
from the amen corner
of chicken and dumpling
memories and places

In my young years
I would have dubbed you
something strange as god
of opiate heaven
of brutal contact
of bible and rifle memories

But the drumhead rolled my name:
How you sound is
who you are
like drumsound
backing back to root
roosting at the meeting place
the time that has always been here

Even here where wood
mates with skin on wax
to make memory, to place us
even in this hideous place
pp-pounding pp-pounding
the ss-sssounds of who
we are even in this place
of strange and brutal design

For B. B. King and Lucille

Hey now, brother, do you
remember? Do you remember
the hurt the anger the contempt
in her eye full of a tear that cursed
your manhood?

Do you remember the slaveship?
Harlem Accra Johannesburg
Bagamoyo! Do you remember
Despair? B.B. is calling your name
Brother! Sister, it is sadness and joy

We are talking about.
The hemorrhage of a continent,
Of the brutality of the sea,
Of men forced to show teeth
Without laughter. Of sleepless
Nights when you turn the light
Off and shudder again
Knowing yesterday today tomorrow again

B.B. knows rats and dues
Knows love knows hurt
Knows hate and your name
Brother, B.B. is calling
Do you remember your name?

Acknowledgement

(*after & for John Coltrane*)

I said a while back
John Coltrane. Trane
And the tracks. What
Womb they lead you to
Is your life nourished,
Or pushed against the walls
Of your festering decay

TRANE, Goodgod, we been
dead so long and missed
the Trane. Listen here:
There is music, will always

be in spite of songs that die
or dry up like crust over any sore

John Coltrane, they say
he died, the hasty fools
that pick his bones for a quick
dollar, John Coltrane, who is
a door, how could he die
if you have ears!

Pro/Creation

(*for Pharoah Sanders*)

Music, as language,
looking in to the world
with the spirit of a people,
identifies itself more precisely
than label. And is there, always,
coming from every place
Pharoah has been—Africa, Asia,
& our long memory in America

He, traveler in sound/spirit,
is direction firm, strong, firmly
connected to root. Expression
past any word. Energies of sound,
old as ear of any god known or not,
now redistributed here to move us
with Love, Morning Prayer, Evening Prayer

Continuities, yes,
the song, memorial and now.
It is from here
Pharoah takes our ear
breaking the silences of our spirit & walls.

Remember slave bells?
And desire? Red, Black & Green;
THEMBI, the woman, home.

For Hughie Masekela

Manboy of the ages
Mirror of my stupidity
And wisdom: yours too
If you know there is no such
Thing as even a perfect god

We are dispensable
Like words or songs
Like obsolete tools
Like your mother's afterbirth

Rending. Yes. We travel.
We move closer. Apart.
Don't we know that even
The sun can be brutal!

This, then is the rhythm
And the blues of it.
Home is where the music is

Places and Bloodstains
1975

Dedicated to the brothers and sisters
who picked up arms to create a
place for us in southern Africa. And
to the brothers and sisters of SASO
and the BPC and MDALI. And to
all African children born anywhere
in the world since the sixties with
the hope that they will not repeat
the blunders we committed.

MAYIBUYE

Requiem for My Mother

As for me
The roads to you
Lead from any place
Woman dancer-of-steel
Mother daughter sister
Of my young years
The roads to you
Lead from any place
I am.
                    I do not know
If you hollered in delirium
Like an incontinent dotard
I do not know if you gasped
For the next breath, gagging
Fighting to hold your life in
I do not know if you took
Your last breath with slow resignation
But this I know

I dare not look myself
In the eye peeled red
With despair and impotent regret
I dare not look myself
In the car groaning
Under these years and tears
I dare not mourn your death
Until I can say without
The art of eloquence
Today we move we move

As for me I will
Never again see the slow
Sadness of your eye
Though it remains
Fixed and talks
Through a grave I do not know
I teeter through
The streets of our anguish
Through this incontinent time and referent
And when I try to Scream *Vengeance*
My voice limps under the cacophony
Of them whose tongue is glued
To the bloodstains in the imperial
Monster's hallways and appetite

As for me
The roads to you
Lead from any place
Though I will never again
Know the morning odor
Of your anxious breath!
Don't let the sun shine
In your arse my child
We do not do those things
Though I will never again
Know your armpit odor
Before the ready-for-work mask
Though I will never again
See the slow sadness of your smile
Under the sun
Woman mother daughter sister
The slow sadness in your eye

Remains fixed and talks
Even here under the amber bandages
Of the sun kiss the day
Before they disappear beyond
These whitehooded mountains and appetites

Epitaph for Can Themba

About mourning,
Many kinds of pictures,
All incomplete,
All the unfinished tapestry at the bottom
Of your old trunk; ...
LEBERT BETHUNE

We think of you as an institution
Demolished by bulldozers of colonial design
We say what does not finish is ominous
So forever like exile is an ominous load
To carry even for one cynical as you
Though we can still not talk of you
As dead. mayibuye!

For all we know
You willed your death
With perverse precision though
You did not invent the spirits
That gnawed at your liver
With the determination of termites
Or the lawandorder which has killed
The mystic dreamer in me

We could have dubbed you fish
But you did not swim in water
We dubbed you CAN as container
And mimicked your decay
Hoping to give birth to our life

CAN child of my mother
"All of you is not involved in this evil business
Death,
Nor all of us in Life."

For Gwigwi

You had a dialogue with death didnt you
Okay you insistent bugger I can hear you say
Come come come come then I want to see
The back of the moon anyway

How could I say
You should not have died
If I believe in life
But your burial was so clinical
Even the green you rested on
Before the machine pulled you
Underground was not of grass

I tried to hear your voice
Hammered to heat of action
Where we stood chilled numb and dumb
I tried to bring back your sense
And sound but nothing came
Except *the years can go wherever*

They want to go I live here
Because you did not trust
This calendar we now use
Without shame as willie
Or boykie american or slowfoot jackson
We left your grave
Open like a fresh wound

Gwigwi in this strange place
Death like any textbook is
A tyranny we participate in
As in any ritual connecting
Our memory to environment
Though we regret it
Like boers or drought of any season
As if it were not to be expected

For TW

How can we say
We shall not participate
In death? How can we say
This ritual is not our own?
But the mouths of fools are here
Like accidents on any road
They will say you have left us
If they offer us the staleness of their
Tears let them. We are not dry
Like wood. We shall not break
Like bone if you live in us
If you live in us
We shall not ask for pity

They will say you were survived
By soandsoandso in ritual delirium
Talking about you as if you are
No more than sentiment. Talking
About you as if you were
No more than body. Talking
As if we are separate like mountains
But as long as we live
We shall do what you did
We shall build children
And homes. Our bodies too
Shall be claimed by the earth
We walk every day. And those with sense
Shall remind us that there is no death
In life only in death. That the old
Know not to ask for pity. That we shall
All participate in this ritual in spite
Of the salty taste of all the pitiful tears
As long as we live

For Otis Redding

Your voice still walks among us
Wherever you are hear us now
Not that when you were here
We were all ready to hear you
Not that the pain in your heart
Was not the bloodstain in my eye
That still kneels at the feet of your voice
But that even the skies are treacherous here

We will not break though
We will again learn to be young
We will move to the reddening of our eye
We will tame and heal the times of eurocentric design
We will reclaim our soil and soul with fire
We will sing the song we must embrace:
I'm names that in dying for life
make life surer than death

Your voice still walks among us
Your memory beckons from the dock of the bay
Through layers of the southland under any sky
Where our soul is red in the soil
Where the young must have ears
Where the bloodstains are not yet dry

Here We Are Like the Present

We met blindly
Lie twins in a womb
When you moved to embrace me
I ran. And that is precise
And brutally true. But fear
Has been known to make people
Do things more strange than
African belief in Jehovah or Allah

Loneliness you say
Leads this parade
So I probe this landscape

This landscape I walk
Is inside like sadness or joy
Though I am the son of NOW
The time that has always been here
But danger, dont I say,
Is not stranger to any time or place
I probe this landscape
Because I come from every place
I have been I know *I love you*
Is as strange as *My mother is a woman*
And here we are
We met blindly
Like twins in a womb
We are here now like dawn or dusk
But where o where is the midwife
To deliver our day or night

Letter to Skunder

Comrade and kind brother
You know the scream of women
Against the brutal tearing of skin
And soul. You know blisters
Deeper than flesh or any god
So shall I put it his way
Your path is no stranger to mine
Go home like your memories

Remember what this Chinese
Sister or brother said a long time ago:
That the birds of worry and care

Fly over your head—
This you cannot change
But that they build
Nests in your hair—
This you can prevent

For Zeke and Dennis

Child of the crisis
Son of sirens knuckles and boots
Tongues pronounce judgment yes
And so do guns and grenades
Armed peace is an act of love
We now know. We now know
—Somewhere a mother will rejoice—

These voices gather
Like rainclouds over the land
We must reclaim. Under any sky
They gather as they whisper in your eye
Or where the smile could have been
Somewhere a mother must rejoice

Wanderer with embers on your tongue
These voices gather to tame
Or fuel the furnace in your eye
On the long road that will nourish soul
And purpose with a simple
THIS LAND IS MINE
Because we now know
—To know our sorrow—
—Is to know our joy—

For Cecil Abrahams

With you I have refound the memory of my blood
And necklaces of laughter round my days
. . . DAVID DIOP

    Mirror of my pain and purpose
    The blood we demand
    Is the flow of life
    We must bleed yes
    There is no birth without blood
    If they call us insane
    Let them. Words will
    Not kill us. If they say
    We are not poets let them
    Our poetry will be the simple act
    The blood we bleed
    Moulded by pain and purpose
    Into a simple
    Do not fuck with me
    Your shit is going up in flames
    Here and now

After Mongane

    I
    I aspire to sound
    leaning on a million
    wretched voices I
    I am this eye
    jumping straight

out of dolphy out of
the sweetness of this pain
open like a mother's thigh
openly I tell you
we are a sacrifice
we are blood of new birth
we do not need love
we do not need tears
openly I tell you I
I am this eye
when you hear guns
my poem will be that sound
hammered to heat of action
in the sweetness of this pain

Son of Mokae

When you open the eyes and say tha
You will say where is the son of Mokae
Bring the bones rootmen
The rootmen say they have fallen like this and like this
There he is he is gone he is gone son of Mokae
Even the oceans he has crossed by planes
The artificial birds of the europeans
He says he is running nowhere he is not fearer-of-enemies
He does not fear europeans bringers-of-war
The evil fools who took our land by force
He says he does not fear them even with nails he could rip them up
He could rip them up without being of feline stock
There he comes the son of Mokae
Manchild fighter-of-war who is sharp is hot

He is hot without being pepper
The war is on young men where are you
Where are you when son of Mokae is looking for you like this
Poet leave him alone you have praised him
You have praised him without knowing his name
His name is spear-of-the-nation

Song for Ilva Mackay and Mongane

Hear now a sound of floods
Of desire of longing of memories
Of erstwhile peasants who can
no longer laugh downhill. My brother
Knows there is no death in life
Only in death. That music is native
So I sing your name

You are child of your tongue
You will be born with gun
In one eye and grenade in the other
You are Tiro: There is no such thing
As escape or sanctuary in life where
All things come to pass when they do
Where every bloodstain is a sign of death or life

You are Mandela You are all
The names we are in Robben Island
You are child of sound and sense
You can look the past
Straight in the eye
To know this season and purpose

You have come from yesterday
To remind the living that
The dead do not remember the banned
The jailed the exiled the dead
Here I meet you
And this way I salute you
With bloodstains on my tongue:

I am not calypsonian
But this you have taught me:
You could say you were from Capetown
Or Johannesburg Accra or Bagamoyo
Newyork Kingston of Havana
When you have come from tomorrow
We shall know each other by our bloodstains

For Montshiwa & Phetoe

it is time to make the time
I see with my skin and hear with my tongue
... HENRY DUMAS

When you see me in misery
It is not tears I lack

Fire ... out of my navel my song
Fire, come bind us. Fire, we aspire
To your elegance. Fire, come burn
These evil maniacs and their vile creations
Fire, it is your impartial evil
And your simple warmth we aspire to

We do not aspire to blackness
That is locked in my navel
We do not aspire to compassion
That we have never lacked
We aspire to sons and daughters
Of postwhite fearlessness and outrage
We aspire to the story
Indelible on my brother's eye
When you see me in misery
It is not tears I lack

And when I reach into my navel
Into the soil that buries my mother
Turned shadow and companion to nightmare
And these eyes reaching for wind
To put fire in our hands
And when fire binds us
Fire of hate Fire of love
Fire out of slime of exile
Fire out of sense and need
Fire of want and demand
When fire binds us
Out of my navel my song

And when you see me in misery
It is not tears I lack

Open Letter

We say what is lost
Into the depths of a whole
We cannot reach by a rod
Is not retrievable
Only the compulsive arrogant
Will want to follow it

Once we were brothers
But that, as Cabral says,
Is no commitment. Relatives
Are not weapons; you cannot choose
Not to be born with one who has
Eyes but practices no habit of sight

What is gone is gone
Remember how it all started
When you like a nightmare
Screamed *cognition* and *prosody* at us
As if we knew nothing of perception and order
You scream in your nightmare now
Or jump from dreams even hard liquor
Could not drown. You will turn on
Whatever light only to find your face
Wet and wonder if home is perhaps
Where the tears come from

The next time
You call me petty or communist
Remember your mother was raped—
Another way of defining relationships

Places and Bloodstains

[*Notes for Ipeleng*]

It's none too soon
to learn the signs:
See that bird over there
Poised on a wingspan
to ride the storm—
the bird knows its enemies:
that's the abc of it . . .
—EZEKIEL MPHAHLELE

You are what you do
beyond any saying of it

For the eye and the ear leaning and groaning
under the weighted centuries of rape and ruin
For the eye and the ear pried open by hunger
by the back peeled raw by the flame and the whip
of bible and rifle contact under any sky
For the eye and the ear wishing and wanting
to rid the slave years of their menace
I lean on the groaning years like the wind
searching their crevices for the life
we came to live

The world remains real
Man and appetite create or destroy
need and want twin parents of demand
where form is a willing servant
of memory and direction
where reason and decision

must destroy illusion
to mother energy and action
to nourish soul and purpose
After birth life must follow
And what you do reflects
nothing but your allegiance

Not that I have been to any mountaintop
where the sun wipes her nose before she shows
or hides her face as any whore. But this I know:

People are not mountains. They will
meet where and if they meet where
the bloodstains are the beginning of birth or burial
Not that the bones that rattle
under the sea could not be your very own
Not that what is eroded
or trampled underfoot and lost
could not become strange or alien
But that the juice that flows
oozes from the fruit or the sore
Not that language could ever be life
But that the hurt that tears laughter
from the eye and gives fire
to the word is more often
a sign of expectations betrayed then hatred
Not that bloodstains are always a sign of death
Ask any mother who has known
sadness or joy

People are not mountains
They will meet where and if they will
Not that there will be no bloodstains

And I repeat it here
while I can see:

> ... *see that bird over there*
> ... *poised on a wingspan*
> ... *to ride the storm—*
> ... *the bird knows its enemies*

In your young years
it is not strange or evil
to be childish. But stay away
from the stench of the childish old
After birth life must follow
and the roads that scar
this earth are impartial or treacherous
therefore I take my brother's voice and repeat:
it's never too soon to learn the signs

Even the ocean cannot claim innocence
the ocean is witness and accomplice
the waves stagger with scattered skeletons
and bloodstains. You cannot cry, though,
all tears taste like seawater

And you, like me,
like any river or creature,
like any season or drum,
will move any and every day
to a particular rhythm
without even thought to it

We live under the sun,
if we do, and die here,
when we do, where all is

collected, collective and old
as childbirth or death

We wish and want
and have tragic memories
though our life is so hideously prosaic
The bitterness of this earth is pawn and parasite
And the elegant tongue is not reliable like the simple act
in the snakepit we are in. Do not lose your mind, though,
or wear it like a wig or damp drawers, like a cashmere cardigan
of a Sophiatown summerday destined for instant death

We also know though
other songs and other places
like the rapid rhythm
when we slip and slide
into and through our jive
like: how could you lose
if you choose the stuff I use
or the slow elegance
when you walk that walk
and carry the meaning
in the rhythm and be
saying, without a word:
Dont it make you feel good!
Though you know that you,
like Ananse, cannot claim
any virginity. Though you
know you don't have to be
a simple-ass whore just
because you have been raped.
Though you know other places
where the bloodstains
don't say anything about rape

After birth life must follow
But now when my voice limps away
from my tongue like a casualty
with bloodstains to testify
under any sky, searching
for the simple act, the re-
assembling of our shattered
and scattered pieces, what
it brings back, riding
the exhausted night which is
treacherous as the sun, as
the whip or the Mississippi
tree where the bloodstains
chronicle this history, what
the voice brings back is a sadsad song

Heartprints
1980

These HEARTPRINTS are dedicated to all our women—our grandmothers, mothers, aunts, sisters, wives, daughters and cousins in our struggle for national liberation and especially to the Women's Section of THE AFRICAN NATIONAL CONGRESS OF SOUTH AFRICA . . .

Letter to Ipeleng on Her Birthday 1976

But daddy I thought you was my main man.
Yes, mama, you know I am, said her father.
Then how come you won't tell me what the teacher
said? I'm sorry Ipe, I was lying. Your teacher said
nothing to me. You know what, daddy? I think it's
about time we stopped lying to each other. (1975)

What is it on your birthday
You want your main man to tell
Your peers who do not have the luxury
Of childhood or the tyranny of fear

How shall I say happy birthday
To you today when young blood flows
Down ghetto and small town streets
Where butcher savages practise their orgies
With jackboots, batons, bayonets and bullets

He is not much older than you
Who said: Father, you cannot go to work
Today, we will need someone to bury us
That, you must know and tell, is fidelity
To life not the slime of deathbound resignation
And your peers do not have the luxury
Of childhood or the tyranny of fear

He was much older than you
Who said: Afrikaans, the language in a laager,
Was not the issue. That is a simple call to
Liberation in our lifetime!

Not that it could ever be without pain
Not that the young skull smashed to pulp
Under fascist jackboots could not be your very own
But that the young blood that flows
Down those ghetto and small town streets
Cannot be in vain

And your peers do not have the luxury
Of childhood or the tyranny of fear

In our land fear is dead
The young are no longer young
The youth call to **Spear-of-our-Nation**
To teach us the way and the means to
Liberation in our lifetime
And you must possess and be possessed
By "a thousand thundering voices
Which call you from the place of the sinking sun"

Because your peers do not have the luxury
Of childhood and the tyranny of fear
Remember this
There is no birth without blood
Liberation in our lifetime
is the only gateway to
Happy Birthday

When the Clouds Clear
1990

The Long Arm of the Blues

Tread carefully among the blues
The blues can be mean

The blues have a long arm
Lean muscular as that of the worker
With more power than memory
And desire. Than a woman's want
Transformed to determined need

The song that saves your life
Could just as readily grab your heart
By the throat. Hurl you against walls
And leave you shuddering
And gasping for breath

The Same Strip of Land

Would-be brother hear me well
This voice I bring you
Is the voice of our mothers
Fathers of my father and your peers
You. . . . . you are your own father

Listen carefully
The ancients say
The finger of the witch
Points at you and withdraws to the witch
But the word that is uttered

Does not return to the tongue
Any more than a deed can be undone

The bridge or strip of land
That allows you to go
Across it to give reports
To those who massacre even infants
Is the same
That keeps some away from home
For years too many to remember
That keeps some away so long
They do not have any memories of home
Though at night they see the lights
Where they dream and fight to return

Hear me well
The voice I bring you
Is not from Moscow
Remember bridge or strip of land
Gets people together or keeps them apart

Listen carefully
When the womb of our mothers
Hears your name mentioned
The womb sings a sad song

Rites of Passage

The roadsigns welcoming the traveller
To Lusaka used to warn us
Do not get there dead
Just get there

We do get weary yes
And die for warmth and tenderness
And so do our children

Do not think the child
Does not have nightmares
Similar to yours

When we get weary
Die for warmth and tenderness
And die in the heat of our time
Wonder if the ice we do not even
Have memory of
Is not stretching its hideous hand
To shake our weary one
Do not think it is beyond the clear grasp
Of the child's anguish
Turned to want and need

Would-be poet stop boring us
With how sensitive you are
Show us what it is
To be man woman child
In want of warmth and tenderness

Dance

Siamese twin
Of song . . . . .
We said a while back
We are music people

In the spell of Tombouctou
We ransack the origin of experience
Stride through the corridors of history and myth
And bounce back to here and now

Mandela Salute Comrade
Thank you for introducing us
To Sankore to Bouctou
Ancient legend vibrant Mali
Meeting point of fact and myth
Amidst harmattan of flower and sand
Where man survives and survives

Morning in Tunis

(for Zweli and Katlego)

Of the paradise and glory
Of the never-ever time
Of a place none can point at
No matter how many preachers are born
There will be no celebration of life
Except where memory collected and collective
From then now and then guides us

Now even though
My children have never known peace
I would like the children of the world
To see with their ear
And sing the sunrise in Tunis

It is heart-of-watermelon red
Mellow like an amber slice of moon
As it emerges from high rock and low cloud
Suspended near the bluesless sky
A spectre between nothing and nothing
Without a single ray of light
As if to simply say
Don't you know the world is remarkable

Sharper Than Any Blade You Know

If I was a bluesman
I'd say
Any day or night
I'd say
Stop messing
With your mama and your papa too
I'd say
Stop messing
With your son and your daughter too

Really are we about to say
Why we so readily
With intention or unwittingly

Hurt the closest ones
More than the ones we hate

For one long summer
More hot more humid
Than a woman's readiness
I was witness
Through window without curtain
Of man woman child and dog

Night after late night
They would walk
In to their open place across the street
Pedro you are a motherfucker
She would say to him
As he lay quiet on the visible bed

Where were Pedro's thoughts
As he kept quiet
Against her torment and want
She would beat him
Violently she would
Later much later
He would get up
And hit back harder
Then Pedro she would scream
Pedro you **are** a motherfucker

In the morning
Pedro wife and child
Quietly walk down the street
Hand in hand
Dog quietly behind them

Who knows
What nightmares they have had

Why do we so readily hurt
The closest ones
More than the ones
We hate

When you try to read or write
If you have the luxury of that compulsion
And your child giggles or laughs out loud
And you scream. . . . .
When you child breaks in
To talk to Mama
While you are listening to your wife
Slicing your idiotic ways
In a tone much sharper
Than any blade you know
And you scream. . . . .

Perhaps you should wonder
If the child is not trying to say
I wish I had different parents

If you are the revolutionary you say you are
Perhaps you should tell us
How happy your family is
To see your face
Any day or night
        Or any time in between.

Bleeding Red

Arrogance is a dangerous luxury
Uninformed it strides our nights
But here in a Tunis hotel room
Italian singers and dancers
Take me home
With the language
Of popular song
In a language
I do not have
The inclination or intention
To torture my tongue with

It is not disco no
It is what I feel for you
Moving deep with gesture of real life
What are words
Compared to sound
Bleeding red with life

Brother places and faces
Can be more dangerously beautiful
Or treacherous than the smile of a child
Or the bloodiest nightmare

When the song of the future
Keeps me awake like a sentinel
It is faces and places I search
I search for language
To arm myself lest I harm myself
As the poet already said

Luthuli Detachment

In the depth of night
My heart is an incendiary
But the flames do not offer any light

Prayer yields no result in life
Programme will and does
As the young say
Tambo give me the machine
That will deliver my day

We must redden
The blackest folds
Of memory and intent

Some say in delirium
That the Luthuli Detachment is ancient detail
Without relevance or meaning now
As if an antique walks among us

You traitor who has defiled
Your mother's womb
With your tongue glued
To the stench
In you master's voluminous bowels
You whose conscience
Is lower than that of the worm
May maggots and red ants gnaw
At where your lifeline might have been
Until the earth stops rotating

Chris Slovo what is conspiracy
If the enemy knows who was between
Whose thighs last night
And has so many children as evidence
What hideous ambush will force us
To name the enemy among our ranks

Questions loom when the lights
Are dark in broad daylight too
Pushing us against the walls of our silence
If our tongue remains tight on the palate
Who are we going to sing as hero of heroes

Oh future memory unbind these tangles
Here now Duma feverish like a dream
With his pioneer eye fixed beyond the menace
Pierces these frustrated walls with the warrior dance
Heita . . . . . . heita . . . . . . Kuth'angihlanye . . . . . . ngihlanye!

Poet do not sedately scratch
The outer trimmings of your voice
When here and now a monster heaves and rustles
Among the flames of an incendiary
More hideous than the end of peace

When the Clouds Clear

She takes no part
In the prime of my slow death
After so many years
She remains foreign
To any form of suicide

Tonight there is no smile
From the remote corners of her eye
Lightning flashes and thunder
Blasts me to smitherings
From the corners of her eye

She takes no part
In the prime of my slow death

Her nerves are stretched irrational now
But stupidity much older than my generation
Or I will ever be
Pushes me into flames where
There is no elegance of eloquence

Oh my mothers and fathers of my father
You who are wiser than I will ever be
Please please tell me
Why is it that my foolishness
Must hurt these loved ones
When the deadly mortars of enemy fire
Are here with us
Every day and night

If you see my back
Wobbling down these mean streets
Without memory or desire
Without fire of hope or conviction
Know I killed the fragrance
Of her hope and desire

What had the ancients observed
When they said of cattle
When I lack it
I have no sleep
When I have it
I still lack sleep
Remember only yesterday someone said
Something makes you do right
The same thing makes you do wrong
Singing about love and happiness

So when we tame this turbulence
It will not be without pain
It will not be without pain
If memory can be witness
And have wisdom
Mother used to say
In the crucible of life
It is what you value most
That will cause the most pain

So when we tame this turbulence
It will not be without pain
It will not be without pain

Or should I just plead
Like the blues singer
Hit me in the eye

Maybe then maybe then
I'll see better
Because when I search the crevices of my voice
I do not want to say anything unreal
As the ancients say
When the clouds clear
We shall know the colour of the sky

Red Song

Need I remind
                        Anyone again that
Armed struggle
                        Is an act of love

I might break into song
Like the bluesman or troubadour
And from long distance
In no blues club
I might say
            Baby baby baby
There is no point in crying
Just because just because I'm not at home

When I try to run away from song
Walking softly in the night
A persistence voice
More powerful than the enemy bombs
Grabs me by the elbow of my heart
Demanding the song
That bathes our lives

In the rain of our blood
Stretched taut in the streets
As Moloise gasps the last breath
Of one solitary life

Should I now stop singing of love
Now that "my memory is surrounded by blood"
Sister why oh why
Do we at times mistake
A pimple for a cancer
And you brother
Who knows our tough tale

Who has been through the tunnel
On this long road
Who has seen the night
Winking and whispering
Who possesses worldwide hands
Of the worker
Who has created
This house these clothes this bed
This street I walk in the night
This light to shatter the darkness of this despair
Tell me why
I must not sing a song of love

Horror and terror are not strangers
When Duma no older than six years
Looks at shoeprints in the yard
And says: Papa who has been here
Rrangwane Uncle Thami Uncle Tim Uncle George
And you do not have shoes like this
Mama why did you leave the window open
The child knows and tells something
About the life we live

So who are they who say
No more love poems

I want to sing a song of love
For the woman who blasted the boers
Out of that yard across the border
And lived long enough to tell it
I want to sing a song of love
Who jumped fences pregnant
And gave birth to a healthy child
I want to sing a song of love
For the old woman who in fearful nights

Still gave refuge to comrades
I want to sing a song of love
For the peasant who shared
His meagre supper with comrades
And gave them shelter
Without returns "for services rendered"

So now with my hands
Clasping guns grenades bombs
Embracing the warmth of my woman's breast
Moving to the rhythm of a mother's love
And the sad sad eye of a father
Embraced in the fixed demands
Of a troubled and expectant people
From the stench of history
And the fragrance of desire and purpose
Softly I walk into the embrace
Of this fire
That will ignite
My song of love
My song of life

From Now On. . . .

(for Debbie and Oscar)

Into the tapestry of the life
We came to live
You weave this unity and union
With the abundance of the love
We come to celebrate and sing

We are the celebrants of this new home
Whose foundation today we witness

Now as husband and wife
Hand-in-hand with one heart
Beating the rhythm of your hope
You stand at the threshold
Of a new phase of life
Which has always been here

The ancients say
Fruit is not a thing
Of the instant
Neither is a happy home
So we offer you our hearts
Our best wishes and hopes
Our desires and our hands
With these make solid bricks
And brick by brick
Together build this new home
Whose abundant fruit
Of happiness and peace
We shall always celebrate
With bold banners
Black Green and Gold
mpilo'nhle

For Olinka

To wander, the ancients say,
Is to see. And, in seeing,
Perhaps wonder about the road
That shapes who we are
Or destroys who we might have been

There then is where
The childhood of our memory
Collected like grain in the harvest season
Or nipped in the bud like seed in the drought

Olinka,
The path of our vision
Of my mothers and kinsmen
Has made you
My pride and joy
Not that stubborn questions
Never invade our restless moments
That is the dangerous luxury
Of the dead of heart and head enjoy

Whether you and I
Or anyone else or creature
Who walk this earth
Believe in any superstition
Native or imported and imposed
Through bible colonial twin of rifle
Is not any of our doubt or fear now

On the day I became your father
A cord powerful as Life's twins

Birth and Death bound us like an oath
In a house some believe
Belongs to some god
Children have not seen build anything
Ask anyone whose home
Is desire and nightmare
Because to be alive
You must have somewhere to go

The sun that rises in the east
And sets in the west
Anywhere on this planet
Also knows
We want somewhere to go
To laugh to love to play
To work to enjoy the life
We came to live

An Injury to One Is an Injury to All

If all the dogs in my country
Were less than dogs, I would say,
Like a Calypsonian, me one, I and I both
Let us dub all our dogs Branch
And that other one
At the Place-of-the-Rocks
Who has disgraced grandmother's womb

We are saying a few simple things here
Like Neruda looking at the blood in the streets

We are saying
Our mothers give birth to heroes everyday
We are saying
Botha's mother gives birth to rats
Every day
Because we hear Killen's Thunder
We say with Langston Hughes
Good Morning, Revolution

Every Patriot a Combatant

Though I do not howl
Like the Wolf
I could go down slow
Like the blues
Or jump back bad
And light fires
To burn down granite
Or toyi-toyi from the future
With the elegance of people's power

Yes Mbeki I know a woman out in Mexico
Whose Zapata heart is worldwide
And heaves with a force
More powerful than the flood

There walks Chris Hani
Across the River Mockba
On his way to South Africa
With the future hammered
To steel in his eye shaping
Every patriot into a combatant

La Guma tell us about the logic of history
About the threefold cord
You weave our spirit into
Here in this stone country
At the fog of the season's end
Where infants with clenched fists
Kick terror in her vampire teeth
Bulalan' Abathakathi!

Quest

If the shoe fits
It might be yours ......
CAROLYN RODGERS

My friend your clear
Voice slashes sleep out of my eyes
Of a night meant for rest
Or the moist warmth of love

In our young years
Your voice had a clarity of its own
Always mingled with tennis balls
Tennis rackets and what the municipality
Wanted us to believe were tennis courts
In townships battling
Against fiends who continue to deny
The right to be human

We grew up as we always will
You aspired to something beyond sport
Your eyes never seemed to be

Where the law and order maniacs wanted them to be
But then as you told me decades later
Your mischievous smile unable to conceal the agony
In your eye inflicted by the betrayal of your quest
'Brother now I play the bottle'
But you and I know
That you will never find
The spirit you want
In any bottled spirits
That change is in the air
All over this country of ours
We both know
That the spirit to move us
To rid our country of every scourge
From Botha to Buthelezi
We will not find in a bottle of spirits
We know past any argument
That an injury to one
Is an injury to all
We should know
Also applies to an injury to oneself
Now we must let blood flow
To give birth to the change in the air
As my brother says
To have a home is not a favour

Kate

And death is the reason
to begin again, without letting go.
JAY WRIGHT

    About longing and lament
    Of a night when a limphearted moon
    Leaks through this humid air . . . .

    And you on the dressing table
    In little sister's room
    Little sister who like you
    Neither knows nor remembers
    Any glamour of youth or exile
    And your eye piercing
    Follows every move we make
    Like an eternal sentinel

    Your death was an end of death
    And here we begin again
    My sister forgive us
    Our demand for the improbable
    Our longing for your presence here right now
    Though what happened on that treacherous road
    And day we know
    Forgive us
    For right now
    It is not you
    But us
    Shrouded in gloom

    My Sister
    I could not come to see

What remained of you
Even if I had dared
I couldn't whiskey my way out of your eye
Any more than I could jump out of my skin
Even on the sixth day
After that treacherous Saturday
That whisked you away from us
I could not come to see
What remained of you

Your spectre patrols my restless moments
When I know I should be slitting fascist throats
Or poeting your determined purpose
But I bounce to impotence like a cheque
Foreign to you in your fashioning our future
I could not even whiskey my way out of your eye
Any more than I could jump out of my skin

Not that it would have made a difference
Had your hasty death on the Morogoro Road been foretold
That was what you had to do
Clearly as a philosophical choice
A meeting though at most of them
There is not much more than platitude or pretension
Clothes for the children though to this day
Most remain as naked as their young souls

So now you are gone
You had to take a final road
Not chosen by you
And finally I came
And I looked
And I was chilled to numbness
A mouth full of cottonwool

Where your weighted smile used to be
Body all shrouded and deathly still
No missile from your tongue or eye
Which always demanded what and why
Later when I wished for rain
To come smother my impotent tears
Baba said
Only the pillow knows the tears of a man

Now like my sister's embrace
Across the treacherous waters and centuries
I want to put my mouth on paper
The poet in me wants to carve
A monument in song
A simple song
Stronger than any granite wall
A song that says
Kate Molale is the people

But the poem won't come

June 16 Year of the Spear

They call me freedomchild
I am liberationbound
My name is June 16
But this is not 1976

Freedomchild homewardbound
With an AK 47 resting easy in my arms
The rivers I cross are no longer treacherous boundaries

Throwing me into the frustrating arms of exile
The rivers I cross are love strings
Around my homeland and me
Around the son and the new day

Who does not see me
Will hear freedomsound
Roaming the rhythms of my dream
Roosting warmly palpable as breast of every mother
Splitting every day and night
Spreading freedomseed all over this land of mine

My mothers fathers of my father kinsmen
Because I am June 16
And this is not Soweto 1976
I emerge in the asphalt streets of our want
And because 'my memory is surrounded by blood'
My blood has been hammered to liberationsong
And like Rebelo's bullets
And Neto's sacred hope
I am flowering
Over the graves of these goldfanged fascist ghouls
All over this land of mine
I am June 16
As Arab Ahmed says
My body is the fortress
Let the siege come!
I am the fireline
And I will besiege them
For my breast is the shelter
Of my people

I am June 16
I am Solomon Mahlangu
I am the new chapter
I am the way forward from Soweto 1976
I am poetry flowering with an AK 47
All over this land of mine

Chimid: A Memorial

Chimid my eye sprung out at the airport
Sprung out of the aeroplane window
To embrace you two years after Berlin
Berlin and Dresden
Dresden when we witnessed
The barbaric destruction of humanity
Screaming through rock and gaping wound
Of stone buildings bespeaking anguished memory

SOUTH AFRICA a poster
Boldly proclaimed in the hands
Of Erdene my Guide and Sister

Where is Chimid!
Anxiously I asked
Being no friend to casual disappointment
The Poet? . . . . . Yes
He died some months ago

Chimid we lie to ourselves so much!
With admirable intent no doubt
We say

Death will not surprise us but
HE DIED....
And speech froze behind my tongue

If I said I felt pain
I would be lying to myself again
I was simply numbed
Even my possible tears
Froze behind my eyes

Chimid need I remind anyone
Who knows life
That death is treacherous
That death is a fascist monster
Who destroys without creating
An alternative you always desired
Who takes without giving
Who surprises us
As if he were not to be expected

Chimid Poet
Creator of manmaking words
Chimid Ulan-Bator Red Hero
Beacon of our future
We shall carve your monumental name
As we fight
For the progress and peace
You wrote and fought for
All over this planet

Seaparankoe

The need of the land we sing, the flowers
Of manhood, of labour, of spring;
We sing the deaths that we welcome as ours
And the birth from the dust that is green we sing
—COSMO PIETERSE—

Malome your body has followed Duma's
In less than the nine months
That follow the blood of the moon
Bidding the mother to usher humanity here

Your body is down under now
Down under Seaparankoe
And predictably there are fools there
Who still cannot know that
The Kotanekind can neither fall nor fail

Our hearts and heads
Remain pliable in the easy embrace
Of your worldwide hands
For generations they will remain
Pliable like dough
Turning to bread
In the worker's hands
Or words turning
To embers of wisdom and courage
At the bidding of the poet's heart

But Seaparankoe the mouths of fools
Who do not know that
No power on this planet
Could ever kill humanity

Or stay our desire for liberty and peace
Are here with us
From the perverse core of their greed

Every person must work or fight
That is the simple truth we learn
From your life and love
Which rules and enhances our vision
Out of the lethal stench of the intemperate present

Here I do not bury or freeze my tears
Salty as the sea accomplice
In the crime and rancid slime
Of pogroms class clashes genocide
Across the taut belly of this planet

Under your vision which commands
Our conscience and consciousness
With easy affection as my brother tells
I say yes to the tears and the sea
I say yes and fashion them
Into the instrument and fruit
Of our informed and determined
Want and purpose
I say yes Malome
We must be bolshevised
I say yes
Every person must work or fight
I say yes
Kotane is dead
But Kotanekind can neither fall nor fail

Come Malome Come
Come we say not that we are dotard

Enough to think we can bring back the dead
Kotanekind come bind us
Come bind the poets
Come make of our music
The sound of the gun
That will set us free
To create to laugh to work
And sing the deaths that we welcome as ours
And the birth from the dust that is green
Not that we are strangers to fear
But we love freedom and peace more
And for this we work and fight

Here You Almost Started

(Care of Rose and Grant)

Who are we to say
This loss is not the way
Of natural balance

Who are we to lay
Blame on fate if blame there be
On any single one or force

You came and you left
Before we could be moved
To laughter or anger or puzzled pain
By the ease of your early infant
Smile or scream or prank
Or impartial focus of eye
Which knows nothing

But that you are here
With eyes that open and look

You came and you left
From the warm darkness of a womb
To the damp darkness of earth's bowels
And that is not different
From anyone's cycle here

You came and you left
You did not stay long enough
With us to know our time
Our limpminded ritual referent
Like Rest In Peace
Rest Departed Stranger
We simply say
We are no strangers to mystery

Rest Departed One
We shall continue
From where you almost started

A Luta Continua

(*Requiem for Duma Nokwe*)

Duma, child of my mother,
Your body has left us, yes
That is a boundary
We had not expected so soon
You taught us, though, that boundaries
And oceans merely separate people bodily

There are men Che said
Who find their hereafter
Among the people
Life and victory as you knew
And lived it in all the "names
That in dying for life
Make life surer than death"
Will continue to flower like your name
From mother's womb and earth's bowels
From hand of warrior and worker too

If the warped bloodhounds of tyranny say
They will torture and kill us
Let them. Let them
Skulls they will crack, yes
Young bones they will trample underfoot, yes
School and church will also try
To twist and break our young yearning minds, yes

But the unbridled brutality of these beasts
Shall not break us. We are not twigs
Your love for humanity and peace
Strengthens us. We now clearly know
A worker's world is ascending

Duma, child of my mother,
There are men who find their hereafter
Among the people
You live forever in us
You are all the names
That in dying for life
Make life surer than death

Poet, leave him alone you have praised him
If you sing of workers you have praised him
If you sing of liberation you have praised him
If you sing of brotherhood you have praised him
If you sing of peace you have praised him
You have praised him without knowing his name
His name is Spear of the Nation. **Mayibuye!**

New Age

The questions which have always been here
Jump at us like impatient lovers
Of nights which cannot be numbed
Not even by spirits departed by bottle or land

When fogs of despair jump up thick in our heads
When struggle becomes the next bottle
Or the warmth between a willing woman's thighs
Sucking into her our hasty greed
Remember O comrade commander of the ready smile
This is pain and decay of purpose

Remember in baton boot and bullet ritual
The bloodhounds of Monster Vorster wrote
soweto over the belly of my land
With the indelible blood of infants
So the young are no longer young
Not that they demand a hasty death

The past is also turbulent
Ask any traveller with memory
To tame it today is our mission
With liberty hammered to steel in our eye

Remember O Poet
When some of your colleagues meet
They do not talk the glories of the past
Or turn their tongues blackwards
In platitudes or idealistic delirium
About change through chance or beauty
Or the perversion you call love
Which be nothing nothing
But the Western pairing of parasites

The young whose eyes carry neither youth nor cowardice
The workers whose song of peace
Now digs graves for the goldfanged fascist monsters
With artistic precision and purpose
Now know the past is turbulent
We must tame it now
Ask any eye fuelled with liberty

Tell those with ears to hear tell them
Tell them my people are a garden
Rising out of the rancid rituals of rape and ruin
Tell them tell them in the dry season
Leaves will dry and fall to fertilize the land
Whose new flowers black green and gold
Are a worker's song of fidelity
To the land that mothered you

Manifesto

This then is our choice and task
Change is going to come

Before the inevitable choice for life
There is only solitude and hungerpang
A lake of pain whose impartial waters
Heave and trace an inexorable path straight
Through centuries dazed by mazes of colonial lies

        Were you there when
        They killed your heroes
        Where were you when
        They killed Lumumba
        And later sold our land
        To vampires from Bonn
        Were you there when
        They killed Lutuli Malcolm
        And the Communist Councilman from Harlem

Yes Mandela we shall be moved and move
We are Man enough to immortalize your song
We are Man enough to root out the predators
Who traded in the human spirit
For black cargoes and material superprofits
We emerge to sing a song of Fire and Love

We emerge to prove again life cannot be enslaved
In chains or imprisoned in an island inferno
We emerge to stand life on her multiple feet
Across the face of the earth

And let no choleric charlatan tell you
It will be by chance
Our voice in unison with our poet's proudly says
CHANGE IS GOING TO COME

South Africa Salutes Uzbekistan

We shall dream yes
And when history absolves us
We shall be celebrants

In sunbathed Uzbekistan
Land of reclaimed desert
The Hungry Steppe now feeds
And clothes land and patriot
And any visitor in solidarity
Under 250 days of uninterrupted sunshine

Here we are celebrants
Sucking the succulent
Ladies' fingers

Tashkent, Samarkand, Soviet Asia
Monument of the past
And beacon of tomorrow
Salute! In the name
Of my people, with my hand
Upon my heart which I offer you
From South Africa and the African National Congress
Good day young pioneers with all
Those flowers and faces for the peace
Your peers have never known in my country

Here we are celebrants of our future
Here we witness the step towards the wholeness
We seek. Here we say YES!
Like the erstwhile Hungry Steppe
Where desert under human hand
Has given up its impartial brutality
For cotton for fruit for flower
For people's power

We are not the sole witness and celebrant here
Vietnam says Yes. Cuba and Chile. . . . Si!
MPLA triumphant and determined beyond
What any Puppet or imperialist monster
Would like to see in this world is here
Here in the land of Lenin
Is PAIGC, PLO and those whose children
Will condemn for having called themselves nonaligned
When the lines of our struggle and choice
Are drawn with mathematical precision

Here we have not seen beggars
We have not seen children
With ribs like guitar strings
To condemn the fat-bellied swine
Who slobber on the dreams of freedom lovers
We have not seen mothers forced to send
Their offspring to any stinking street
To peddle human juice for meal or drink
Here we have not seen the humiliation of tyranny
The fear the loathing of oneself
Which my brother has known and told
Here man will live and flourish
Yes Uncle J.B.
Yes Malome

Yes Dadoo
Sisulu, Fischer Yes
With clenched African National Congress
Fist for people's power and my small hand
Upon the banner for the peace we must fight for
Yes

Salute Tavarishee, we are celebrants
Of your present and our future
Amandla! Comrades. As Castro knows
History will absolve us
YES to electrification
YES to irrigation
YES to industrialisation
YES to desert reclaimed
YES to solidarity
YES to freedomsong
YES Lenin, We shall dream
We shall turn that dream into reality
Palpable as this cotton this flower
This fruit this love
MAYIBUYE!

To the Bitter End
1995

To all my comrades who have fallen. And especially . . .

To the memory of Alex la Guma

MY KROON

The world dont belong to General Motors

The world dont belong to Chase Manhattan

The world dont belong to Coca-Cola

No matter how cool the pause that refreshes

To the memory of Cass:

Nna ga ke phoko, ke

Pheleu magatsa'nku

Ram, you live among the people

To the memory of Thami:

I say with bitterness

To the memory of George & Lindi:

Moe'nie worry

boet Smoko?

To the memory of John Motshabi:

In the stillnesses

of the night

I wonder what made you

Jump out of your coffin

To the memory of Johnny Makathini

Mfanafuthi my brother

Six feet under

At Leopard's Hill

Is a long way

From home. By why

My brother why

To the memory of Zakithi

Hayi, S'bari, intoni ngathi

Uyimbongolo ngoku?

Coil of Time

What Time Is It?

For seventy-seven years
Rainclouds have been gathering
Around my heart
    COME THUNDER!
Come even on a clear day
      Come pierce
The swollen womb of these clouds
Let the rain rage and rave
Come Thunder
   COME HAILSTORM

If Home is in the furnace of the womb of my eye
If Home is where heart and head always are
I am the man on his way home
If peace is exile
If peace is moving North and North
We do not want peace

In the Wheeling and Dealing Time

Kinsman how will the crimes
Of our land be purged
These days these intemperate days
Sometimes I wonder though
I'm no bluesman
Sometimes I wonder
Just what it is
Or where it is we are going to

Are we headed for the light
At the end of the tunnel
Zinjiva has already seen and sung
Moved to behold flowers with our mothers
Or are we headhunters
Headed towards the chilling nightmare
Of an inexorable conflagration
These days
                These intemperate days
                            Sometimes
I wonder
                Sometimes ... no ... often
These days I feel I should jump bad
Because as my brother says
Daar is kak in die land

Rites of Passage: (1991)

(*for Uriel 'Thabang' Mabitse 'Papers'*)

Your time on time
Has creased history's arse
There are no crossroads
Your passage through here
Teaches us weight of mission
Teaches us slime of promise
From mouths greased with stench
Of crimson dollar or rand
Or whatever currency demands
Floods of your blood
All over this land
You must reclaim

In this world
There are no children's wars
You are man now
Patriot and comrade now
You now know
The slime of race
You now know
The brutality of class appetite
You now know
Who must bleed and drown
In the fire of your mission
And resolve
                    IHLOMILE!

Dumalisile

(SOMAFCO 10th anniversary)

YES I am Solomon Mahlangu
Always the way forward yes
Yes death could never silence me
My blood will never be mute yes

I have outlived nights
And endless days of agony
I have outlived more terror
Than the maddogs of this world can unleash

The song of my blood has caressed
The calloused and withered hands of the old
woman
Who in rags washes the robes of her torturers

everyday
The song of my blood is in the mines
In a plate of food
In that page a window into life
In the street that erupts with violence or love
The song of my blood
Is in the mind and passion of the youth
Whose eye has been reddened by determined
resolve

They tried to remove me from speech
They tried to exile me to silence
But my song elegant as the rainbow
Thunders on a clear day
Piercing the eardrum of their arrogance
Like the spear of my ancestors
The same spear that the sons and daughters
Of my song pierce the enemy
Of their childhood games with
As they dance to the memory of days to come

Bana ba thari e ntsho
Kana bangwe 'bo ba ka mpotsa
Gore gatwe kgangkgolo ke eng
Ba itira okare ga ba itse
Gore nna ga ke utlwane le gobalabala
Kana ga ke monna ke mosimane
Ke tla siamelwahe ditsame sentle fela
Ka ke sa leke goipagololela megodu

I am the children of the future
I come dressed in the rainbow
Of the flames of my song
Didnt you hear my brother say

White people must learn to listen
Black people must learn to talk
Kalushi is talking now

Do not mourn me
I am a celebrant here

I Am

Beware my friend
I might be millions or more
Things than what you have convinced
Yourself I am
    I am what
     I am
Without apology or hypocritical regret
When sound grabs me
And hurls me into the heat of music
I can be a Coltrane Coleman Dolphy solo out there
And deeper than any word you know
Probing and exploring
Every crevice and slice of life
From now to all pasts
Presents and any plethora of futures
To bring you edibles

I can be tree
Loving branches swinging
In the arms of wind
Luxuriant leaves in their green laughter
With the sun

I could be an infant
Teardrops at the eyelash
Without a word
Challenging you
To name the reason
Behind the tears
Since you say you know it all

I could be maddog willie
Annoyed past any saying of it
By an idiotic question like
Don't you think there is a danger
That the ANC might be misguided
By the Communists

Then I could be the ghoul
In your nightmare
Which hurls you out of bed
And sleep wet with cold sweat
Because you have just heard
That Communists and terrorist monsters
Have taken over the country and they say
The land belongs to those who work it

Of a night in Cape Town
I could be that angry young comrade
Who insists through his liquor fumes
He democratically wants things a certain way
Who insists clean your place first democratically
Who does not democratically realize
His place is not too clean

I could be CAP
Through the tongue of my walls

Saying it is time we took art
Out of the galleries
And on to the streets

I could be that crazy
Little South African poet who insists
That the heights or flights of
Artistic exploration
Or the depths that any
                    Artistic expression
Might plunge into must
Be dialectically related to
                    Social relevance

I could be Nadine
Insisting that the writer
Must seriously handle language
Through the texture of life

I could be millions of what
                    I am
Just as
        I am
                Just as
I am

Manboy

Oh I
   I might not be
Sterling's ubiquitous preacherman
Who just visits visits Chitown
But sometimes borne on the wing
Of the fastest lightning
I visit childhood
To meet me naked
Where I was born

There smiles that plumpy little boy
Whose nimble eye is veritable sunshine
Kneaded into a slice of joy
More commanding than the orders
Of a military command any where

There whirls that energetic runt
Whose pranks are foreign to fear
Or are so readily fearful of possible punishment
Approaching him through expression of face
Or tone of voice of mother
Who is now neither
Confidant
               Nor trustee
                 Nor ally
That he soaks himself in piss and tears
Sometimes the childhood possesses
And with ease carries heavy files of memory
Which open without a creak
Frightening me with knowledge I must now
reclaim

Like when I overheard grandma
Telling a neighbour
'MaSemangmang you must stop
Sending this child when he has seen
You doing nothing when the others
Would not be sent by you
You will make him a stubborn monster

Oh I
I might not be
A frequent visitor to that child
But I have never turned down
An invitation to childhood
Though at times even in clear daylight
I have met nightmare there

When the Deal Goes Down

So now you have become increasingly reticent
It's a long way from the warmth
Of a loving and loved parent
Whose hugs and kisses and mischief
Carry love and care and laughter
Palpable as flowers as a loaf of fresh bread
To this pensive young voice

Papa everything has a reason right

You are stunned to thought
The child is talking dialectics
And you fear what might be coming

You fear that you do not know
Perhaps, you say to the child
But . . . say . . . what are you saying

You know Papa some times you come home
Tense and impatient
One little thing we say or do
And you threaten to punish us
You yell at us you tell us
You have had enough of our nonsense

Alright do you think there are times
When I have a reason to do that
O-o-o-oh plenty of times
Okay next time when there is no reason
Promise you'll let me know

We dream in our quest
Determined past any argument
To reclaim ourselves our Home
Is the dream thereby insulated
From nightmare which looms and leaps at us
Through the child's anguish
Which has ambushed her laughter

We do not have a mother
Mama is always away
Struggling to liberate us
When she comes home
It is only to sleep

Scientific though you say you are
You feel haunted by uncountable demons
Pounding you amongst the walls of your haggard

despair
And the young voice now barbed
And intractable deflates you

I do not know my father
Papa is always busy
He does not know me either
I pick up pieces of my father
From all the uncles I meet
In search of him
Who is my father
I try to fit these pieces together
To give birth to my father

The clear voice that sees you
With the power of collective memory
Slices the core of you and you shudder
As you hear

The vice is getting tighter
And you're standing in between
No place to hide
No place to run

Your whole being is a trapped tangle
And you gasp shuddering again
In the heat of your cold sweat
Reeling and wading through the stench
Of your dream turned juggernaut
And you scream
     rescue me*!*
To nobody that you know
To no force you could name
In the moment of when the deal comes down

Years without Tears

When like Neruda
I do not know
Where home is
When like Neruda
I know only the face of the earth

When I cannot answer
When you ask
When was thus-and-so
When I know only that
Time is always stubbornly now
And you say
I am naive
And perhaps you say
I am stupid
I will accept

I will accept because
You do not know how the blues
Mold dues paid into a fireflood of joy
Even if you heard man or woman
Upon seeing father forced to be
Witness to mother and daughter raped
You would want to know why
Their voice sometimes feels like a motherless
child
Or why that voice says
Sometimes I wonder
I wonder whether I'm a man or a mouse
Or why that woman over there
Has never loved any man good to her
The way she loves her heartbreaker

Though you have eyes
That open and shut
No child needs help to know
You have no habit of sight

Though I know
I possess no voice of wisdom
I know the blues like children
Like sunrise like sunset
Were born before us and borne
Through we will all die
And leave them here

Strange Rituals

Your leg lives apart
From your land
Which mothered you
What memory breathes
Through its muscle
Which directs it
Back and up and down
We do not know

In your nimble abandon
Perhaps you believe
You are might without
Sparrow black bird in flight
Or sparrow in delirium
Without might of flight
On the wingspan of a dream
Headed nowhere

I son of my son
Son of my daughter
Father of my mother
Child of all ages and people
Waded through this miasma
Children say is your breath
I knocked at the door of your dance
When the door swung open
I did not see any person
Perhaps I could not see you
All I saw was leg swung
Back and up and down

I courier of my daughter's
Precocious mischief
Allergic to the stench of any shit
I correspondent of People's Ethos
Eager for the scoop on your epoch
For my Party's Working Class Intelligentsia
Bulletin
Risked my health and possible sanity
In the thick of your miasma
I opened my mouth and ripped silence apart
Perhaps you are too far out to be visible
Could you without platitude
Tell us what your mission is

Grand Papa Dhlomo

Do I have your permission
To peep through the heaving crevices
Of your heart
In search of my voice
Which might not always name
The specific strains of its quest

Baba you romantic old sorcerer
Colt that I have been
In my young years I roamed
Your valley and hills
Robed in the splendour
Of your thunderous voice
Like a streak of black lightning
Wrestling to tame this strange tongue
From across the big waters
All the eyes of my tongue
A blazing torch anxious
Searching for all the women
Who are the woman you love

Now that the idealist in me
Limps like a horror out of a cave
With the callouses inherited
From the cause of this romantic quest
You did not warn us against
I would simply like to know
What you made of our idiocy
Which embraced your mischief
As the profound depth of life
Heaving and intensely lived
Without pretension

For David Rubadiri

Every fella is a foreign country says
My sister who is an area
Of mellow feeling and catharsis
Who can rage and rave like the blues
Or like la Guma's preacherman
Across vastnesses of land and water and memory
Who knows *the world dont belong to*
General Motors
The world dont belong to Chase Manhattan
The world dont belong to Coca-Cola
No matter how cool
The pause that refreshes

Now though I am
Neither scientist nor philosopher
I know there is something of you
In Rubadiri of the slow smile
Who can explode into folds of laughter
Or the tears you can feel in the depths
Of his heart. Like you Rubadiri is
A foreign fellow he is you
Rubadiri can ask a diplomat who talks
Can you make a baby smile
Rubadiri can ask any man
Do you know how it feels to be pregnant
Of a sunday morning straight from service
Where he has been scratching his jaw sedately
Rubadiri can ask
In a tone juvenile mischief would envy
You know bhuti they talk as if
Sugar daddies are a thing of now
But Joseph the father of Jesus
Was he not the original sugar daddy

For Bra Ntemi

Isn't sound continuity
Isn't sound memory
Loving care caress or rage
Sticking our shattered or scattered pieces
together

Marabi is a filthy memory
Marabi is talent stomped in stokvel
And smothered in skokiaan fumes
Yet and still
Who would have been Mbaqanga's midwife

Bra Ntemi
What does a man bring to music
I wax back to the rebirth of our sound
Willard Cele
                        They are zombies now
Whose dance does not go back
To the birth of our new sound
Township passion screaming for space
Screaming for breath
Screaming for a moment of life
Raging and raving in the wilderness of our day

Oh Bra Ntemi have you not paid your dues
From Gallo to now!

Fidelity

(For S.O.B.)

And every day and night here in Chicago
I know past any argument
That I am the man you will never kill
Because I am the son of the blues
I'm Billy Branch I'm Carl I'm Mose

Hear now here now
Here we come
Here we say
He was such a good man
Why did he have to die
In Vietnam in Angola in Namibia
Or anyplace anytime in the talons
Of inhumanity

Is Billy Branch the fire of the blues
Raving and roaring all up in flames
Or is the blues Billy Branch afire
On the stormiest monday
Any ear has ever flirted with
Molding my sister here into the sun
Whose rays are the arms of her eye
Caressing me with the seductive power
Of a mother's inimitable smile
Bathed in the sweetness of the pain
Known only by those whose autobiography
Testifies to the pitfalls of loss and love hugging
In the crucible of life

And here now
Is this why my brother Serote
Who has beheld flowers
Serote who knows
No Baby Must Weep
Has already told us
It is a tough tale

Montage: Bouctou Lives

Even nature at her best
Is singing her mesmerizing beauty
With the permanent rainbow
That is the wonder of Mosioathunya
Says nothing of the woman of Mali

My Mali sisters are a rainbow
Even the deaf and dumb
Would aspire to sing

Here Keats would have found voice
And song instead of the finality
Of deadness
He dubs beauty and love
Though we do not see human gesture
Nor life in his Grecian urn

My sisters of Mali could
      Teach any rainbow
           The impartial beauty
                Of nature through a rainbow
Of centuries of memory and mutations

Look at the flow of that ebony elegance
Walking that walk
Striding through your heart
Turning Bamako into a dream
And that blue-eyed ivory contrast over there
That strut is a vector on the graph
Linking Africa to where
And all of that all in
Between bespeaks where

Which woman have you not met here
In Mali I have seen my mother
My daughter I have seen
My grandmother and her very own too
My wife friends comrades
All the women I love and hurt
All the women without whom
I am not even here
All the women without whom
Neither you nor I
Could claim an identity
Which all that lives has

I wish I had enough
Art of eloquence and grace to sing
The woman of Mali

Heart to Heart

Without even vaguest thought to it
They suddenly clearly know
They could never have a love affair
Such vulgarity would be an attempt to return
Some place they have never been together

They are not in love they never will be
They simply love

The rhythm of her legs
Walking towards him is song
The call and response of life
Itself is her eye engulfing all of him
And when her lips touch his
Heart to heart
They drum to the same beat
Oblivion takes over the world

And Fire from now on
From this moment on Fire
They are not consumed no
They are a streak of black lightning
Through layers upon layers of song

Without even the vaguest thought to it
They now clearly know
They could never have a love affair
Perhaps now like Mayakovsky
He is not even a man
He is a cloud in pants
They are not in love they never will be
They simply love

Poet T'under go drop I'm telling you
I did not say I could build castles
Out of any single grain of sand
But I have spoken
I mouth that tells no lies
Have spoken don't I say

Your eyes she says are looking out
Searching but at the same time she says
Your eyes are searching looking in

We Are All Involved

(*for Cheryl*)

Though I have never claimed
      I could sing
      I am a songwriter
      I do not have to think
To know that I cannot return
Where I have never been

As Nti puts it at the end
Of wherever he may have travelled
I will tell you straight
When stubborn scientist assaults poet
For seeing with Jean Toomer
Africa's goatpath where Georgia pike
Comes from or when
Poet insanely tramples scientist underfoot
To submission all up and down and deep
My meness becomes grass
Violated beyond any possible green

But always these two enemy friends
Defy the most possible death these two know
There is no such thing as finality
In the space they share these two know
Even death-at-birth is where we always begin
again

Though my intelligence is derivative
And my depthoffeeling the selfsame way
I claim the right for the imprint
Of my impulse hollering or moaning
Or murmuring through this terrain
Like Carl's Mississippi guitar
To name its specific identity and quest

My sister thank you for your presence
As simply human without apology
Full of love and hate and fear and courage
Without a catalogue of what some call reasons
I love you as simple as that

O Earth I could say
I could say Wind
Water and again Water
I say Fire
O Fire unbind me
Unbind me I want to sing my name
My brother knows I see with my skin
Knows I hear with my tongue

Even Skin Disappears

WHERE he feels
        He might explode
        To smithereens

But here don't we know
There are no enemy explosives
Which reduce one to tiny
Strips of biltong scorched
And clinging to walls and trees

Where no part of the body
Is recognizable from any other
Here boundaries between two people
Disappear. Even skin
As everything else disappears
Even thought takes leave of absence

There are no separate identities here
The sword in the ceiling of her thigh disappears
Language itself rendered speechless disappears
Where would any naming of this new arrangement come from

If I Could Sing
2002

To all our mothers, daughters, wives, sisters,

'the rock-hard foundation of our struggle,' as Madiba correctly says. As

long as any woman remains any patriarch's 'occupied territory' *A Luta*

Continua! Malibongwe!

And to the memory of

Baba Mabhida, Ntate Mashego, Tata O. R.,

Comrade Shope, and Chris Hani.

May your eye condemn us

till the end of time if we ever betray our mission.

Recollections

Spring up and advance
Or retreat
Into and out of memory
You think you have finally
Started on a decisive journey
Away from the Africa of colonial design
Along with that of the narcissistic poets

You pause
Here
In search of direction
If your destination remains
Elusive
How do you propose
To know what direction to take

Though you remain
Convinced
To be alive
You must have somewhere
To go
Your destination remains
Elusive

Habits of movement rattle and peep
Through the silences
Surrounding your memory
As they ambush
What might have been

Clarity of in- or fore-sight
Or thought
But did you not only yesterday
Say where to go is what to do

Dizzy says:
It's taken all my life
To learn what not to play
How long will it take you
To learn what not to say?

Venceremos

Says Consolata our lady
Of the soft vision
The gaze of the blind:
I will teach you
What you are hungry for
                Thank you Toni
So questions jump up naked and agitated
Pushing us into the tightening vice
Of inconsolable memories
Demanding resolution

In love we are a quest
As in the rest of what
We are most responsive to
We must know though
The road to fulfilment
Is never   s
               t
               r
               a
               i
               g
               h
               t

I love you you are mine
Must never be allowed to mean
Anything about ownership or submission

I love you you are mine
Must mean fellow traveller
We are celebrants
Like the mother who knows
Sadness and joy
Like any birth it will not be
Without the tearing of tissue
Ask my sister who fears
The end of peace who knows
Where the kind kills are

We are like this poem
A quest and a sacrifice
So even when we bite lip in anguish
Even when a response or its absence
Threatens to mock our dream to abortion
When we find out as Ornette
Who is griot who is dreamkeeper
And the very way forward
When we find out we can
Make mistakes we will know
We are on to something
And this is why and how
The blues jumps clean out of pain
To immerse us in a vibrant celebration
Of life

Poet leave it leave the heart alone
It has depths words will never reach
Leave it alone to wander as it will
To its heights of ecstasy
Or its depths of contemplation
Like the blues

Affirmation

The sound of her voice
Weaves a song with meaning
Past the depths of any word
That might try to name
Or bridle and tame it

In the sound of her voice
I remember every thing
I will never forget

Love might not be all
That a person needs
But it does count

Here with my little hand upon
The tapestry of memory and my loin
I once again lean on the blues to find voice:
If loving you is wrong
I don't want to do right.

Memorial

Though we know
Life is no long joy
Someone enters your life
And stays there

You learn
Something about desire
And learn to live here
What is revealed is subtle
Though quiet it is equally intense
A flame not red but blue
Its contours vividly simplified and softer
Once here you seldom want to leave

When you stumble upon stillnesses
And such curious spaces without warning
You think you miss your old place
Where memories stayed within immediate reach

You now have difficulty finding memories
It is perhaps the lack of history
Yet peeking at you
Are images of beginnings
That have become soft remembrances
You turn over and over
Wondering at their comfort

If I Could Sing

I want to remain
Wild
Like a young song
Unleashed
Aspiring
To the serenity
Of a Japanese morning
Hour
In which not a single leaf
Stirs above
Water stone and tree
If I could sing
Like Neruda I would
Weave a song about
The size of your worldwide heart

Renaissance

I remount the curve of evil times
to unearth my anchored memory
ABDELLATIF LAABI

Again I say
I am music people
the cadence of what
we are moved by and move to
informs my eye
which does not want to risk

even a blink
for fear I might miss

some essential gesture
of the life we must live
in all its robustness
and sing as hours here
or any where we choose
breaking through all the silences
in the crevices of our turbulent memory

soundman
that I have always aspired to be
my ear sees the tentacles
of our fragile voice
breaking through the walls of our exiles
as I remount the curve of evil times
to unearth my anchored memory

Rejoice

Says Thebe Neruda of the vibrant smile
The eye so curious it is reluctant
To shut the world out even in sleep
I am the dreamkeeper he says
The spontaneous song and the dance
Pulsating with the force of my people's ethos
Watch me
                    And rejoice

Our sister Betty Carter
Repository of our memory
Whose mouth is free of all untruth
Who plays her voice as a horn
Says you can do anything
You want to do
If you know what to do

I am witness and celebrant here
I do everything I want to do
Because I know what to do
I am the dreamkeeper I say
The mouth that tells no lie
I am not a man
I am a boy
Beneficiary of the fruit
Harvested from my people's memory
Watch me
                    And rejoice

Poet leave him
Leave him alone
You have praised him
You have praised him
Without knowing his name
His name is Mouth-that-tells-no-lie

This Way I Salute You
2004

For Johnny Dyani

When I swim in my music
a harmattan of colours
becomes an area of feeling
where a rainbow of feathers
peoples all space
dancing in my heart

Here I do not even know
what flowers pop out of my eye
I move
        without even touching air

Johnny you take us out there
where we gasp silently
amidst a bombardment of sound
in the spell of the witchdoctor's son
where I cannot even ponder
how a witch and a doctor paradox
could be one entity

Your bass
Johnny pins nothing down. Your bass
rides on wave or height or rock
or depth or crevice of sound
to bathe us in music

And we are moved
where we cannot even
hear ourselves gasp

Santamaria

Is where the vowels dream
in a name among consonants
chasing the crevices of sound
in a ritual longer than the distance
between the shores of the ocean
which cannot expose its hideous memories
Refusing to be blinded by sea water
Mongo is not from the Congo
but on conga or any drum
Mongo gathers all our memories
like the crop of an abundant harvest
from the oracle of his palms
and commands them to the bidding
of the polyrhythmic dance of life
He whose hands speak
a people's ethos on skin and wood
sagging with memory and resolve
is a sacrifice like the *son*
Poet, what words could have
the eloquence of his hands at work or play
to nourish your life

Cassandra Wilson Will Sing

Let me sense the chaos
I will respond
with a song
why else
was I
born
says Jimi of the purple haze
through Kalamu ya Salaam

Now look at those eyes
look at her arms
follow her little finger

I wonder what
Jean Toomer who could see
the Georgia Pike growing
out of a goat path
in Africa
would say about
Cassandra Wilson tonight

Perhaps Cassandra
does not even sing
Here of course a voice there is
possessed by music like the rest of her
her whole body is song
her whole body has sensed the chaos

I say look at those eyes
look at her arms
follow her little finger
and understand perhaps why
you were born with ears

Where Her Eye Sits

After reading Cheryl Harris's *From the War Journals*

Follow me where her eye sits
and gasps reddened with unthinkables
and a song saying a few simple things
already seen like Neruda like
come see the blood in the streets

Follow me where her eye
now reddened has travelled this slippery road
littered with empty pockets and festering hungers
indelibly stamped with the eyes of children
and generations

Follow me where her eye
sits and sees disembodied bowels
skulls scraped clean of matter
bones that rattle without the shaman's magic
bones whose determined rattle is a remember
and reminder who cannot be wished away

Follow me where her eye
sits and says
where to go is what to do

eThekwini

(for Edessa and all the poets and celebrants: Poetry Africa 2002)

I plunge into language
hoping to emerge with the shout
or whisper of the quiet and secret places
my sister celebrates
the tender and blue flame
of her voice moving us
deep
in
to all that we are
or could be. Here we must

jump to recreate ourselves where
Keith Jarrett warns us, there's no way
to practice jumping except by jumping

Like any child you know
I grow. When they ask me then, since
I have been to these big waters here
how does the tree in water grow
will I know what to say?

Here amongst the sounds
of the ocean, the river that moves
like the dancer, and the hills
whose back you must ride
any where you want to go,
I have met the whole world
in motion like this ocean

For Gloria Bosman

Her face is like an ancient cameo
Turned brown by the ages
LANGSTON HUGHES

And Langston Hughes' eye
must have embraced Gloria. How
else could he have said her beauty
burns in my heart a love-fire sharp like pain

And if I could I would
borrow a million voices
to sing her name

She who gathers the whole world
into the body of her soul
and immerses it
in a moment of sound
vibrant as cleansing ritual
and sacrifice

Her head she throws
back
the rest of her in steady
motion with all the force
of the rhythm section

If you want to be loved
without restraint come along
Gloria Bosman is not afraid
to take risks. She is into something

Gloria Bosman will bathe your heart
in the flames of her song
as she plunges into every crevice
of all that is her
possessed like a medium
her million voices exploding
love is in the music

For Our Mother of the Heavy Names

Tsamaya sentle—mama, walk good

Ipuseng—
We must fulfil
the mission
your name commands

Galekgobe—
Life will not sap us
of our energies
for we shall create
and create

Arwa—
Valiant comrade of the Red Sea lands
did you not teach the English a lesson

Our mother of the heavy names
though this is your visit
you are not a guest here
neither of honour nor of any other

sentimental shaping or ordering
of this day or any other reality
we experience and know

Our mother of the heavy names
walk good
you are not the sole celebrant here
we claim your joy as ours
and though I know I cannot sing
nor play my voice like a horn
the way Lady Day always does
I celebrate all the arrivals
of peace
        from the future
        I see
        dancing in your mischievous
eye and smile today

Homesoil in My Blood
2018

To the memory of Phyllis Ntantala and Ken Simmons,

Weavers and architects of the fabric of our being

No Boundaries

I possess neither wings
nor the magician's mischief
but, believe me, I can fly;
and I can also be a landscape
of mirrors that name whatever moves
or has pretentions to be alive.

On the wingspan of my desire,
easy as the approach of any day,
you can clearly remember
I can fly to any place
or moment fertile with memory
or create fresh ones without a single boundary
though our lives remain so pathetically prosaic.

With informed hope
and resolve we must know
how to move forward to a landscape
where our dreams cannot be turned into nightmare,
where our dreams are always in sight,
where we must again
redden the blackest folds
of our memory and intent.

No Serenity Here

An omelette cannot be unscrambled. Not even the one prepared in the crucible of 19th-century sordid European design.

When Europe cut up this continent into little pockets of its imperialist want and greed it was not for aesthetic reasons, nor was it in the service of any African interest, intent, or purpose.

When, then, did the brutality of imperialist appetite and aggression evolve into something of such ominous value to us that we torture, mutilate, butcher in ways hideous beyond the imagination, rape women, men, even children and infants for having woken up on what we now claim, with perverse possessiveness and territorial chauvinism, to be our side of the boundary that until only yesterday arrogantly defined where a piece of one European property ended and another began?

In my language there is no word for *citizen*, which is an ingredient of that 19th-century omelette. That word came to us as part of the package that contained the bible and the rifle. But *moagi*, resident, is there and it has nothing to do with any border or boundary you may or may not have crossed before waking up on the piece of earth where you currently live.

Poem, I know you are reluctant to sing
when there is no joy in your heart,
but I have wondered all these years
why you did not or could not give
answer when Langston Hughes, who
wondered as he wandered, asked:
what happens to a dream deferred

I wonder now
why we are somewhere we did not aim
to be. Like my sister
who could report from any
place where people live,
I fear the end of peace
and I wonder if
that is perhaps why
our memories of struggle
refuse to be erased,
our memories of struggle
refuse to die

we are not strangers
to the end of peace,
we have known women widowed
without any corpses of husbands
because the road to the mines,
like the road to any war,
is long and littered with casualties—even
those who still walk and talk

when Nathalie, whose young eyes know things, says
there is nothing left after wars, only other wars
wake up whether you are witness or executioner—
the victim, whose humanity you can never erase,
knows with clarity more solid than granite
that no matter which side you are on,
any day or night, an injury to one
remains an injury to all

somewhere on this continent
the voice of the ancients warns
that those who shit on the road

will meet flies on their way back,
so perhaps you should shudder under the weight
of nightmares when you consider what
thoughts might enter the hearts of our neighbours,
what frightened or frightening memories might jump up
when they hear a South African accent

even the sun, embarrassed, withdraws her warmth
from this atrocious defiance and unbridled denial
of the ties that should bind us here and always
and the night will not own any of this stench
of betrayal which has desecrated our national anthem
so do not tell me of NEPAD or AU,
do not tell me of SADC
and please do not try to say shit about
ubuntu or any other such neurosis of history

again I say, while I still have voice,
remember, always
remember that you are what you do,
past any saying of it

our memories of struggle
refuse to be erased
our memories of struggle
refuse to die.

my mothers, fathers of my father and me,
how shall I sing to celebrate life
when every space in my heart is surrounded by corpses?
whose thousand thundering voices shall I borrow to shout
once more: *Daar is kak in die land!?*

Letter from Havana

(*For Baby K*)

A while back I said
with my little hand upon
the tapestry of memory and my loin
leaning on the blues to find voice:
If loving you is wrong
I do not want to do right

Now though I do not possess
A thousand thundering voices
like Mazisi kaMdabuli weKunene
nor Chris Abani's mischievous courage
as I trace the shape of desire and longing,
I wish I was a cartographer of dreams,
but what I end up with is this stubborn question:
Should I love my heart more
because every time I miss you
that is where I find you

In the Naming

We now know past any argument
that places can have scars
and they can be warm
or cold or full of intrigue
like faces.

Since the settler
set his odious foot here in 1820,
my Caribbean brother might say,
these hills have not been joyful together

In Rhini you can go up
or down or any direction
in the lay of the land where
the people have memories as palpable
as anything you can see with your own eye

But in Grahamstown,
those who know say,
any where you go is uphill

Anguish Longer Than Sorrow

If destroying all the maps known
would erase all the boundaries
from the face of this earth
I would say let us
make a bonfire
to reclaim and sing
the human person

Refugee is an ominous load
even for a child to carry
for some children
words like *home*
could not carry any possible meaning

but
displaced
border
refugee
must carry dimensions of brutality and terror
past the most hideous nightmare
anyone could experience or imagine

Empty their young eyes
deprived of a vision of any future
they should have been entitled to
since they did not choose to be born
where and when they were
Empty their young bellies
extended and rounded by malnutrition
and growling like the well-fed dogs of some
with pretensions to concerns about human rights
violations

Can you see them now
stumble from nowhere
to no
where
between
nothing
and
nothing

Consider
the premature daily death of their young dreams
what staggering memories frighten and abort
the hope that should have been
an indelible inscription in their young eyes

Perhaps
I should just borrow
the rememberer's voice again
while I can and say:
to have a home is not a favour

Wounded Dreams

Amongst the silences of restless nights
My voice wants to break through the shell of words
to name and sing the evidence
of our resolve and will to live
past the glib claims of noble intentions

If you have never walked through
the restless shadows of wounded dreams
beware; the young ones of tomorrow
might curse you by not wanting to remember
anything about your ways because everything
about you leaves a bitter taste in the mouth

Amongst the silences of these restless nights
our dreams refuse the perfumed bandages
that try to hide the depth of their wounds
Our voice yearns for the precision to name
what we are most responsive to
the way our lady of the mutton vindaloo
of my demand said: *Listen here,
Shorty, this is hell's kitchen
you'll walk out of here tall you hear*

Though the present remains
a dangerous place to live
cynicism would be a reckless luxury
toxic lies piled high and deodorized
to sound like the most clear signage
showing us the way forward from here

Not that I am dotard enough
to think it could ever be easy
or without pain to do anything
of value. But when I am surrounded
by the din of publicly proclaimed multiple promises
I wonder if we can say with determined resolve
like Fidel: *Never again will pain return*
to the hearts of mothers nor shame to
the souls of all honest South Africans

Though the present is
a dangerous place to live
possibility remains what moves us
we are all involved
indifference would simply be
evidence of the will to die
or trying to straddle some fence
that no one has ever seen

together we can and must
rehabilitate our wounded dreams
to reclaim and nourish the song
of the quality of our vibrant being
as evidence of how it is to be alive
past any need for even a single lie

Out of the silences
of these restless nights
my voice wants to break
through the shell of words
and fly to the rooftops
to shout: when we have walked through
the restless shadows of wounded dreams
and come back from tomorrow together
we shall know each other
by the root and texture of our appetite

I Am No Stranger

I am no stranger
to confusion
though I concede
there are people with wants I seem
not able to understand any more
than a child could grasp any talk
about abusive parent or dysfunctional family

My brother ZP tells me it is my lack of certain
appetites that denies me the clarity I seek
I do not possess the street philosophy of Langston Hughes'
Semple who could explain anything from the uniqueness
of his shoes to Virginia the woman or the state

Once I thought
I had a friend but she asked me
eyes blazing beyond the heat

of any fire you have ever known:
What does your wife have that I do
not have. *My love*, I responded
thinking she wanted an honest answer

When I walk through Guillen's Grand Zoo
I wonder what he would have named
this animal whose want turns
into urgent greed easy as
sunshine in the summertime. Or
is that my confusion at work again?

We Are All Involved (2012)

I walk through afternoons, I arrive
full of mud and death,
dragging along the earth and its roots
and its indistinct stomach in which corpses
are sleeping with wheat,
metals, and pushed-over elephants . . .

says Pablo Neruda
whose home is the face of the earth

The dead will not remember
the devastation of Haiti
the dead will not remember
the impartial brutality of nature
that ravaged the land of Toussaint

The dead die with all their memories of death

If you claim to be alive
your memories of Haiti
must haunt you
if you are not dead
you must remember
there are people
with urgent needs in Haiti

We are all involved

Under the sun
that will rise and set
with a familiar ease
anywhere you might wish
you could escape to
you have no right or authority
neither moral nor legal
to feel helpless even against
the brutal might of nature

My brother says death is the reason
to begin again, without letting go

We must rebuild Haiti

Of Shadows and Chameleons

Don't I say again the present
remains a dangerous place to live
and now at the risk of trampling
on some sadistic toes who might
want to hurl words at my face
to sting like toxic waste
I want the young to see
that the present is littered
with the debris of our gangrened dreams

When we seek harmonious resolution
when we want diversity
even at our expense instead
of the solidarity that informed
our resolve to turn our dreams
into life full of the laughter of a people
who have somewhere to go

When we settle for the rigid
compliance of an unimaginative bureaucrat
where, then, oh where is the morally conscientious voice
to cup the poisoned vein of the present that sags
under the brutal weight of these insatiable appetites

Who will teach the young that
our memories of struggle
cannot be erased
our memories of struggle
refuse to die

Festive Heart

(for Baby K)

The festive heart knows
it is always possible to do more
of what you must do
and do it better, always

When Mingus says
he is going to play
the truth of what he is
he is not playing games

Neither is Sun Ra
when he says
he actually paints pictures
of infinity with his music

And so I know it is
always possible to do
more of what you must do
and to do it better, always
because the difference that a day
might make celebrates the day
that makes the difference

I know also there are scandals here
some open and loud
others closed except for
their hideous stench

So when you see me walking up
or down these streets

singing your name
it is because I'm happy
to bury the loneliness
some call freedom
as I embrace this moment where
Love leaps and soars
beyond any familiar height
or imaginable horizon
painting pictures of infinity
as it plunges into every crevice
of this festive heart of mine

I Know a Few Things

My sister who knows
that just trying to stay alive
in the streets of Chitown
is like guerilla warfare says
if the shoe fits
it might be yours

My brother says
silence is death by default
and so I know I am alive
because it is my voice
that startles me now with
DAAR IS KAK IN DIE LAND

And I wonder about
what some might want most
because they believe it to be valuable

or what they believe is most valuable
because their brutal appetite wants it

In this age of hope
for some the present remains
a dangerous place to live
What do you name the distance
between
what you have done
and
what you know
you should have done

Someone please tell us
what is going on

It was only yesterday
it seems
when the future
that could be read
in our determined eye
did not have words like

alleged rape
like violence against women
or brutality against children
or consensual sex with your daughter

Here now we hear
a slimy attorney might urge
a child violated to
withdraw
rape charges
with the perverse ease

his fucking friend
withdraws
his sinister penis
after shuddering with the brutal force
of his ejaculation

Look in those young eyes
if you dare
condemning your depraved ways
with a determined
what the fuck is going on?

New Day

Your limp mind
cannot see that
what you do
defines you with a precision
no words could evoke
in any language

Let me put it bluntly
without any art of eloquence:
though you say you are a man
your perverse ways refute that claim

In any language
you are clearly not human enough
to be a man. Even as
the brute you are
you cannot be called animal

as that would be an insult
to any beast that ever walked this earth
you are not a man
you are an insult to every mother's womb
you are the rancid poison
that ravages what could have been
home, as sanctuary

Beware
the new day is here
Hear the wisdom of the ancients:
What has no end is ominous
freedom from fear of violence
is neither favour nor privilege
our determined resolve to live
and sing the freedoms that are ours is here
as my sister might say:
You think you are a cancer
But we know *you are a pimple*
we will squeeze you out

The new day is here
to spread laughter
with much warmth and care
the new day is here
and we shall celebrate it
365 days every year that comes
without fear of violence
from now on

For Fernando, Gloria, Eduardo and the 2012 Team

Could those whose eyes
blinded by greed and other appetites
too ominous to name understand when
the poet says: *I am from everywhere I have been*
but you without need nor desire for pretension
know I must be from Medellin

I sing your name for bringing me
to the city of flowers and the whole world
from its aboriginal roots to its troubling present
and the richness of life gathered; diverse and vibrant
every eye focused on the heartbeat
that make us one, simply human

I sing your name
for bringing Medellin and the world
that we must rediscover to me
to keep moving to the rhythm
the poet names a vibrant aesthetic
defining and affirming life as creative
alive to the fire of what it is to live
without need nor desire for pretension

I sing your name
for weaving our resolve and voice
into this 22-fold cord that will
not be broken by the monsters who want
to plunder the womb of the earth for profit

For Sterling Plumpp

When Harriet Tubman
heard the thunder of the guns
and saw their terrible lightning
and the blood and the dead bodies
your voice was there

Your voice was born and borne
in the muddy waters of the delta
way before a brother had been
through enough to resolve
he would rather drink muddy water
and sleep in a hollow log
than go to New York City
and be treated like a dirty dog

Sterling, we dub you itinerant
as troubadour here to testify
when your mojo hands call
we must go to reclaim our history
and resolve that no force on this planet
will ever fold our life into banknotes
as we create our future full of laughter
and purpose

As Baraka says: we own the night
and the day will not claim them
how could you not testify
when your voice is parent
and son of the blues

For Hu Xiancheng

Our sister of the determined passion
and clear vision taught us that it is
better to die on your feet
than live forever on your knees

And now my brother's eye
sears through the squares
and rectangles that shape
and order our lives. From birth
certificate to death certificate and the grave
we are squared in and squared away

Someone please tell me where
our circles and cycles of life
went. Are now doubled
or are we pathetic duplicates of others?
Or have our deities left home forever?

Uncollected
1971

Carbon-Copy Whiteman or Sexual Refugee

In the corridors of your mind
Fulsomely flattered by Ivy League or Oxford
Delirious with flat-assed long-haired irreality
Glib fancy of self-emasculation
Would-be brothers, how
Do you plan
To placate this fury this
Black light
Scorching everything anti-human, civilising man?

Is your waist-deep conscience
an experimental death
a fear of being Self
a slave brainchild of European refugees
thriving in the ghetto of your mind?
Is enslavement between white sheets a modern ethic
or simple rose-tinted glasses on your twisted head
up in the crotch of your natural enemy
an obvious concentration camp for imitation whitemen?

Check this out
Even the seasons of the year change
Day yields place to night
The sun is setting on your soul.

The Awakening

My sleep was like a prenatal death.
After 300 years I thought something in me was awake
But then I couldn't have been awake
Because nothing sounded clear—
Nothing sounded good enough
Unless it had a white background.
I flirted with Marx
Kept my ear open to Tshaka,
Moshoeshoe, Dingane, Garvey, DuBois.
Then came Nkrumah's voice,
Heraldic of bearings flowery as spring.
Lumumba, Kenyatta, Mandela, Sobukwe,
Kaunda, Babu, Castro, Tour, Mao—
Twentieth century recipe
For a grass roots favourite dish.

Then I came to America,
Twentieth century capital of the living dead
Petulant whores fighting to make me a phallic assimilado
A sexcessful relic of the house nigger.

Amidst sit-ins, kneel-ins, sleep-ins and mass mis-education
Brother Malcolm's voice penetrated alienated bloodcells
Teaching Black manhood in Harlem USA
Endorsing "Bandung,"
Retrieving Black balls cowering in glib Uncle Tomism
Forcing me to grow up ten feet tall and Black
My crotch too high
For the pedestal of Greco-Roman Anglo-Saxon
adolescent Fascist myth.

Now I see everything against a Black background
As Black and proud as Melba
Breaking the blood-dripping icons of Western congenital
    chicanery
Enthralling me like the cataract of a cosmic orgasm.

Manifesto (1971)

After the inevitable rebirth
There is only loneliness a necessary pain
As quiet as a deep lake
Whose waters from the eternal spring
Trace a straight path
Through the maze of centuries of colonial dreams
Awakening
Overturning
        (Were you there when
        They killed your heroes
        Where were you when
        They killed Lumumba
        Were you there when
        They killed Brother Malcolm)

'Yes, Mandela, We Shall Be Moved'

Yes, Mandela, we shall be moved
We are Men enough to have a conscience
We are Men enough to immortalize your song
We are Men enough to look Truth straight in the face

To defy the devils who traded in the human Spirit

For Black cargoes and material superprofits
We emerge to sing a Song of Fire with Roland

We emerge to prove Truth cannot be enslaved
In chains or imprisoned in an island inferno
We emerge to stand Truth on her two feet We emerge

To carry the banner of humanism across the face of the Earth

Our voice in unison with our poet's proudly says
'Change is gonna come!'

Fruitful Seed (1971)

Almost lost on slippery snow
I say I was almost frozen
In cold white, icy tired
      I descended into my soul
      Where a torrid torch melted the snow
      And healed beast-inflicted wounds. Now
Tirelessly I bask in the sun

And sour up on my cloud
Pregnant
Married to Nature I see me as me
Dancing with the wind
Cocoa delight, precious
South African diamond
    Instructions for freedom road
        MAUMAU!

Freedom Train, 1965

Freedom train chanting
Freedom train gaining momentum
On revolutionary wheels . . . Yes,
The wheel is revolving
All my children taking a freedom ride
From Dixie to Congo . . .
                (Charlie, faster now
    I don't want to miss that ride
    How many lives do you owe me
    Your unquenchable bloodthirst
Possibilities of glare in the Congo, Cuba
South Africa and more! Oh yes,
I have read
Your twentiethcentury bloodbath synonyms
Compiled in your parthenons vaticans pentagons
Because your gods' godlessness
Is an unholy phallus of doom
Fucking with material death
Your slime polluting wouldbe Bandung spirits
Bloodstained bills can't buy you exoneration)

I've got instructions from my brother,
Said, take care of business, brother
You've got nothing to lose but your patience
On revolutionary wheels

Freedom train chanting
Freedom train gaining momentum
All my children taking a ride
And the wheel is revolving

Introduction to a Future History Book

(*To Sun Ra*)

Dark clouds race across the earth
for the final flood. Beat
the frenzied rhythm
give birth to Life
stop the years from groaning. I
have known unseasonable filth
fly with Sun Ra
to sunlit regions cleansed by soul units
turn mythscience into a reality. Like
carry your heat and burn
every infernal chain in the furnace of your life
you have nothing to lose but fear
do not go west, young man
do not go west
it is a pale monster-infested shithouse

SOURCE ACKNOWLEDGMENTS

The editors would like to thank the following sources who first shared Kgositsile's work and who granted permission to reproduce it:

Spirits Unchained (1969) is reproduced by permission of Broadside Lotus Press.

For Melba: Poems, copyright 1970 by Keorapetse Kgositsile, is reprinted by permission of Third World Press Foundation, Chicago, Illinois.

My Name Is Afrika, copyright 1971 by Keorapetse Kgositsile, is used by permission of Doubleday, an imprint of the Knopf Doubleday Publishing Group, a division of Penguin Random House LLC. All rights reserved.

The Present Is a Dangerous Place to Live, copyright 1974 by Keorapetse Kgositsile, is reprinted by permission of Third World Press Foundation, Chicago, Illinois.

Places and Bloodstains (1975) was first published by Achebe Publications.

Heartprints (1980) was first published by Schwiftinger Galerie-Verlag, East Germany.

When the Clouds Clear (1990) was first published by the Congress of South African Writers.

To the Bitter End, copyright 1995 by Keorapetse Kgositsile, is reprinted by permission of Third World Press Foundation, Chicago, Illinois.

If I Could Sing (2002) is reproduced by permission of NB Publishers (Kwela Books).

This Way I Salute You (2004) is reproduced by permission of NB Publishers (Kwela Books).

Homesoil in My Blood (2018) is reproduced by permission of Xarra Books.

"Uncollected (1971)" is reproduced courtesy of Baby Kgositsile.

Exodus
'Gbenga Adeoba
Foreword by Kwame Dawes

After the Ceremonies:
New and Selected Poems
Ama Ata Aidoo
Edited and with a foreword
by Helen Yitah

The Promise of Hope: New and
Selected Poems, 1964–2013
Kofi Awoonor
Edited and with an introduction
by Kofi Anyidoho

Modern Sudanese Poetry:
An Anthology
Translated and edited
by Adil Babikir
Foreword by Matthew Shenoda

The Future Has an Appointment
with the Dawn
Tanella Boni
Translated by Todd Fredson
Introduction by Honorée
Fanonne Jeffers

There Where It's So Bright in Me
Tanella Boni
Translated by Todd Fredson
Foreword by Chris Abani

The Careless Seamstress
Tjawangwa Dema
Foreword by Kwame Dawes

Your Crib, My Qibla
Saddiq Dzukogi

The January Children
Safia Elhillo
Foreword by Kwame Dawes

Madman at Kilifi
Clifton Gachagua
Foreword by Kwame Dawes

Think of Lampedusa
Josué Guébo
Translated by Todd Fredson
Introduction by John Keene

In the Net
Hawad
Translated from the French
by Christopher Wise
Translated from Tuareg
(Tamajaght) into French by the
poet and Hélène Claudot-Hawad
Foreword by Hélène
Claudot-Hawad

Beating the Graves
Tsitsi Ella Jaji

Keorapetse Kgositsile:
Collected Poems, 1969–2018
Keorapetse Kgositsile
Edited and with an introduction
by Phillippa Yaa de Villiers
and Uhuru Portia Phalafala

'mamaseko
Thabile Makue

Stray
Bernard Farai Matambo
Foreword by Kwame Dawes

The Rinehart Frames
Cheswayo Mphanza
Foreword by Kwame Dawes

Gabriel Okara: Collected Poems
Gabriel Okara
Edited and with an introduction
by Brenda Marie Osbey

Sacrament of Bodies
Romeo Oriogun

The Kitchen-Dweller's Testimony
Ladan Osman
Foreword by Kwame Dawes

Mummy Eaters
Sherry Shenoda
Foreword by Kwame Dawes

Fuchsia
Mahtem Shiferraw

Your Body Is War
Mahtem Shiferraw
Foreword by Kwame Dawes

In a Language That You Know
Len Verwey

Logotherapy
Mukoma Wa Ngugi

When the Wanderers Come Home
Patricia Jabbeh Wesley

*Seven New Generation African
Poets: A Chapbook Box Set*
Edited by Kwame Dawes
and Chris Abani
(Slapering Hol)

*Eight New-Generation African
Poets: A Chapbook Box Set*
Edited by Kwame Dawes
and Chris Abani
(Akashic Books)

*New-Generation African Poets:
A Chapbook Box Set (Tatu)*
Edited by Kwame Dawes
and Chris Abani
(Akashic Books)

*New-Generation African Poets:
A Chapbook Box Set (Nne)*
Edited by Kwame Dawes
and Chris Abani
(Akashic Books)

New-Generation African Poets:
A Chapbook Box Set (Tano)
Edited by Kwame Dawes
and Chris Abani
(Akashic Books)

New-Generation African Poets:
A Chapbook Box Set (Saba)
Edited by Kwame Dawes
and Chris Abani
(Akashic Books)

New-Generation African Poets:
A Chapbook Box Set (Sita)
Edited by Kwame Dawes
and Chris Abani
(Akashic Books)

New-Generation African Poets:
A Chapbook Box Set (Nane)
Edited by Kwame Dawes
and Chris Abani
(Akashic Books)

To order or obtain more information on these or other University of
Nebraska Press titles, visit nebraskapress.unl.edu. For more information
about the African Poetry Book Series, visit africanpoetrybf.unl.edu.

CPSIA information can be obtained
at www.ICGtesting.com
Printed in the USA
LVHW111728091222
734905LV00004B/174